ns PROGRAM

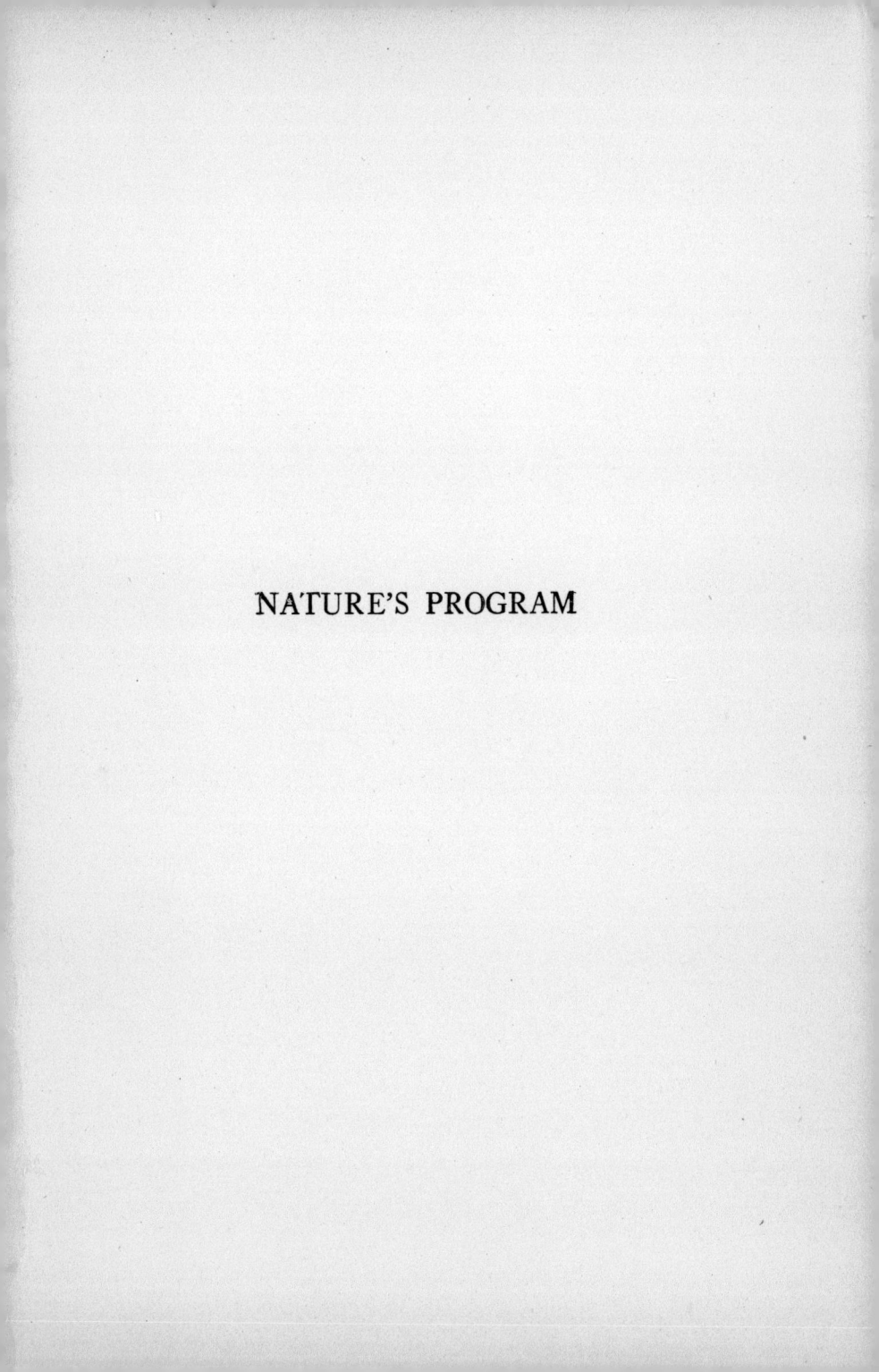

The NATURE LIBRARY

NATURE'S PROGRAM

By
GAYLORD JOHNSON

DOUBLEDAY, DORAN & COMPANY, INC.
GARDEN CITY   NEW YORK

COPYRIGHT, 1926, BY NELSON DOUBLE-
DAY, INC. ALL RIGHTS RESERVED.
PRINTED IN THE UNITED STATES AT THE
COUNTRY LIFE PRESS, GARDEN CITY, N. Y.

NATURE'S PROGRAM

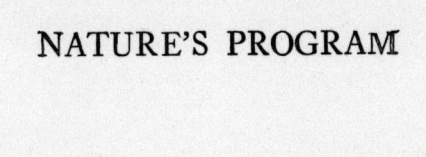

How To Use The Pageant of Nature

When you go to the theatre you want to know, before the curtain rises, where the different scenes of the play are laid, and who the chief actors are. The theatre program gives you this information. You may lose some of your enjoyment in the play if you do not know some of these things beforehand.

In the same way, if you are going to enjoy the year-long spectacle of Nature to the utmost, you want to know who the bird, animal, insect, flower, and tree actors are, and a little about the parts they play in the continuous performance whose separate "acts" are the months, and whose "scenes" are laid in the woods and fields. It will make your pleasure in the outdoor pageant far greater if you know, before you start out upon your ramble through the country or the city park, just about what you may expect to see.

You therefore need a "program of Nature" to tell you at what time of the year, and in what places, you are likely to find the different birds, butterflies, animals, and plants. That is why this book has been prepared.

It was designed as a supplementary volume to the newly revised *Nature Library*, which consists of six volumes, one on Birds, one on Wild Flowers, one on Butterflies and Caterpillars, one on Trees, one on Animals, and one on Garden Flowers. These volumes contain a vast wealth of fascinating Nature lore, with hundreds of illustrations in color to enable Nature lovers to identify wild creatures and plants easily. But it was felt that many "amateur" Nature explorers would miss most of the ever-fascinating events that occur in Nature, if they were not forewarned about them. Accordingly, to supplement the *Nature Library*, this little guide, "Nature's Program," was prepared. But although it is a supplement, it stands upon its own feet and may be used to great advantage even by those who are completely ignorant of Nature's phenomena. Naturally, however, to obtain the greatest benefit from it, and to be enabled to get the greatest enjoyment from Nature, it should always be used in connection with the *Nature Library* or with some other reliable and complete series of Nature books which the reader may possess.

In other words, this guide to the events of the year has its natural limitations, and they should be clearly understood. In the first place, it is obliged to confine itself largely to what is most dramatic in Nature and what Nature explorers take most delight in—namely, the *first appearance* of plants and creatures. When flowers can be found throughout several months they are listed under each month. Birds, however, which, after migrating, remain resident for several months, are listed only in the month when they first appear in North or South. Butterflies also are, as a rule, mentioned only in the month in which they first appear, although they are usually to be found on the wing all through the summer season.

Then, too, it must always be remembered that this book is *only* a guide, and it can be nothing else. It can warn you *when* to look for the different birds and butterflies and flowers. It can tell you *where* they are most likely to be found. But it cannot help you in identifying them, nor can it assist you in understanding the interesting processes by which Nature works its thousands of marvels.

In using this book, also, it will be well to remember *that the time-table of Nature's procession of monthly events is not inflexible.* It varies somewhat, depending, in the spring, for instance, upon whether the snow vanishes for good and all in early March, or whether it holds on

HOW TO USE PAGEANT OF NATURE

until April. The times of appearance, as well as the varieties of animals and plants themselves, will also of course vary somewhat with the part of the country where you live. The dates of first appearance have, however, been apportioned from the careful notes of reliable Nature students, and will be found true for the average year in the latitude of New York City. They will be found to vary three weeks or so between the northern and southern boundaries of the United States.

Because it cannot be anything more than a guide, the best way to use "Nature's Program" is as follows: Before you go on an outing, glance over the month. You will find itemized the most interesting things you may expect to find. Some of the common flowers and birds you may know well enough to identify without assistance. But you will find mentioned many rarer creatures and plants, and often the most interesting ones, with which you are not familiar. Under each item you will find a reference to the page and book of the *Nature Library* where a full description is given, with complete and interesting information, and in many cases a full-page illustration in color. Pick out a few interesting things you want to seek that day, and read about them in the *Nature Library* or in any other reliable Nature books you may have. Then go forth to find them.

In other words, go into the woods and fields intent upon finding *something in particular*—be it bird, butterfly, or flower. You may not find that particular thing that day, but your eyes will be sharpened by your expectation and purpose, and you will at least be certain—if you do not find what you are seeking—to see something else just as interesting. Then when you get home, if you have discovered something you had not expected, look up in the books the creature or plant that you *have* seen.

As a famous Nature student puts it, "Don't go into

the woods as if they were a kind of Noah's Ark; for you cannot enter the door and find all the animals standing in a row. You will go a great many times before seeing them all."

And don't think you must always walk in a new direction. *Go often to the same fields, the same woods, and become very familiar with them.* You may not see so much the first time, but each succeeding walk will show you things you missed before. When you get to know every fence corner, every stump, every pile of stones, you will find a hundred interesting things that you never dreamed were there on your first visit. Mr. Dallas Lore Sharp, the well-known writer upon Nature's everyday doings, says that when he went to live on his little farm, it did not appear like a very "birdy" place, or very full of animal life, yet he finally found the nests of thirty-six species of song birds within five hundred feet of his house, and eventually made the acquaintance of forty-six woodchucks, all living in holes on his fourteen-acre property!

So even the small city park may prove a better place to study Nature than you suspect, and there, or in the real country, a little preparatory knowledge will open your eyes to the keen pleasures that only a close acquaintance with Nature can bring.

March, The Wakening, or Crow Moon

The Indians, to whom Nature's program of the year was an open book, named each month for the most striking event taking place in it. So March, with its first stirrings of flowers, trees, and animals from winter sleep, was the "Wakening Moon."

For the nature lover, March is truly the dawn of the year. Even in its first days, when patches of snow still cover the ground in the woods, you will be quite likely to come upon the very first blossom of the spring. You may find it even in the first week of this month, piercing the melting snow in a boggy spot.

It does not look much like a flower; just a purple-streaked hood pushing up through the cold mud. But wait a few moments, and you may have unmistakable proof that it is indeed a flower. If you are fortunate, you may see the arrival of your first bumblebee of the season, as she hums about the door of the

The Skunk Cabbage

"skunk cabbage," and enters to obtain her first load of yellow pollen. The bee's visit proves this humble prophet of returning spring to be a true blossom, even though it may lack both colored petals and pleasant perfume.

But if you insist that your first blossom of spring must be a "real" flower, you will probably have to wait two or three weeks for the appearance of the hepatica, or liverwort,

"Whose just opened eye
Is blue as the spring heaven it gazes at,
Startling the loiterer in the naked groves
With unexpected beauty; for the time
Of blossoms and green leaves is yet afar"—

Of course the hepatica has many rivals for the honor of being first upon the scene of spring. Some nature-lovers have found the yellow violet, the spring beauty, the wild ginger, the anemone, the trailing arbutus, or the bloodroot —before they have seen the hepatica. But when you know that a trustworthy authority has found it blossoming under a foot of snow in December, you will probably be willing to grant it the prize for promptness. Unless winter is abnormally late in taking his departure, you should find the hepatica and many of its rivals before April comes.

The Hepatica

But while you are keeping an eye open for the first flowers, do not grudge attention to the trees, for they, too, are preparing, in their own way, to welcome the spring. In March the bare, angular limbs of the aspen show green under their bark, one of the first prophecies of spring; then the buds cast their brown scales and fuzzy gray catkins are revealed. There are few textures of silk and velvet that are not rivalled as the catkins lengthen, and dance like chenille fringe from every twig of the aspen.

And perhaps, even in March, you may come upon the starry magnolia, covering itself with star-shaped white flowers; or the flowering dogwood saluting the still bare woods with its creamy beauty.

MARCH

During bright days in late March you may even see one or two kinds of butterflies on the wing in open glades of the woods. Do you know what they are, and why they are able to come out so far ahead of the varieties that will wait until May and June to appear?

You should also be alert in March, the "wakening month," for the appearance of those animals which sleep or hide through the cold months. The badger generally appears above ground as soon as the snow disappears, and the regularity with which the cheerful little chipmunk appears above ground in the first warm days of spring has often been remarked upon. Some chipmunk, mounted on a log or root, starts a loud, chirpy "chuck-chuck-chuck." Others, as if only waiting the signal, rush from their holes, and add their loud and vigorous cries to the spring salute. Did you ever hear how the little Indian boys used to take advantage of this responsiveness of the chipmunks?

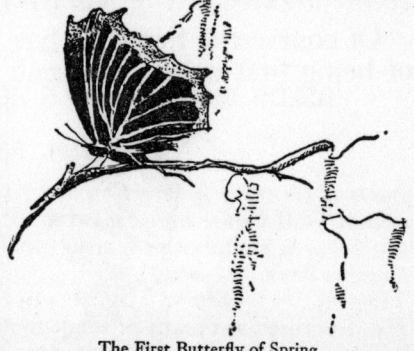

The First Butterfly of Spring

In March, too, if you live in the North, your eyes may be gladdened, and your ears thrilled, by the return of the first birds. Even before the snow is gone comes the bluebird; and soon after the brisk, vociferous robin.

The Bluebird

Do you know what material he uses for his nest, and how it differs from the homes of most other song birds?

Nature in March, the "wakening month," is so full of interest and excitement for the nature lover, that we can no more than touch the "high spots" in this quick survey. Find, in the lists below, the subjects about which you feel most curiosity, and learn all about the delights of March in the fascinating pages and full-color pictures of the *Nature Library*.

BIRDS MIGRATING NORTHWARD IN MARCH

Blackbird, Red-winged

Parts of Country Where Found: North America east of the Plains, except Gulf Coast and Florida. Breeds from Ontario and Quebec southward; spends the winter chiefly south of the Ohio and Delaware valleys.
Times of Appearance: Migrates north in March; south in October.
For description, means of identification, strange wholesale courting habits, nest, food preferences, etc., etc., see page 127 of The Nature Library volume on BIRDS.

Bluebird

Parts of Country Where Found: North America from Nova Scotia and Manitoba to Gulf of Mexico. In winter from Middle States to Bermuda and West Indies.
Times of Appearance: Migrates northward in March; southward in October. A few sometimes remain throughout the winter in the North.
For description of appearance, habits, nest, food preferences, reason why the bluebird is the symbol for happiness, kind of houses to attract them with, etc., etc., see page 21 of the Nature Library volume on BIRDS. For color and identifying marks see full-color illustration facing page 18.

Cowbird

Parts of Country Where Found: United States and British America, from coast to coast. Spends winter in Southern States and Mexico.
Times of Appearance: Migrates north in March; south in November.
For article on habits, food preferences, nest, colors of plumage, description of appearance, reason why it often lays eggs in other birds' nests, etc., etc., see page 129 of the Nature Library volume on BIRDS.

MARCH

Dove, Mourning

Parts of Country Where Found: North America, from Quebec to Panama, and west to Arizona. Most common in temperate climate, east of Rockies.
Times of Appearance: Migrates north in March; south in November.
For article on food preferences, nesting habits, why these birds' married devotion has become a proverb, etc., etc., see page 201 of The Nature Library volume on BIRDS. For color, appearance, and identifying marks see full-color illustration facing page 210.

Finch, Purple

Parts of Country Where Found: North America, from Columbia River east to the Atlantic, and from Mexico to Manitoba. Most commonly found in Middle States and New England. Spends winters south of Pennsylvania.
Times of Appearance: Migrates north in March; south in November. Rarely, individuals winter in the North.
For description, means of identification, why the name is not accurate, nesting habits, food preferences, etc., etc., see page 117 of The Nature Library volume on BIRDS.

Grackles, Purple and Bronzed

Parts of Country Where Found: Purple grackle: eastern U. S. from the Gulf to Mass. Bronzed: North America east of the Rockies, breeding from the Gulf to Hudson Bay and Labrador. Spends winter in southern U. S.
Times of Appearance: Migrates north in late February and March; south in October.
For article on habits, food preferences, nest, colors of plumage, description of appearance, why song is compared to a squeaky cartwheel, etc., etc., see page 121 of the Nature Library volume on BIRDS.

Hawk, Marsh

Parts of Country Where Found: North America in general, nesting throughout, but wintering only in southern half.
Times of Appearance: Seen from March to October in northern half of country.
For description of appearance, habits, nest, food preferences, why farmers should encourage it to visit their fields, etc., etc., see page 195 of the Nature Library volume on BIRDS. For color and identifying marks see full-color illustration facing page 195.

Hawk, Sparrow

Parts of Country Where Found: Eastern North America, from Great Slave Lake to northern South America. Nests from northern limit of range to Florida; winters from New Jersey southward.
Times of Appearance: Permanent resident the year round south of New Jersey. Seen in North from March to October.
For article on food preferences, nesting habits, strange method of hunting, benefits conferred upon farmers, etc., etc., see page 184 of the Nature Library volume on BIRDS. For color, appearance, and identifying marks see full-color illustration facing page 174.

Killdeer

Parts of Country Where Found: Temperate North America to Newfoundland and Manitoba, nesting throughout range; winters usually south of New England to Bermuda, the West Indies, Central and South America.
Times of Appearance: Migrates north in March; south in November or later. Most abundant in migrations.
For description, means of identification, how to tell a flock of them while in flight at a distance, habits, food preferences, etc., etc., see page 213 of the Nature Library volume on BIRDS.

Kingfisher, Belted

Parts of Country Where Found: North America, except where the Texas Kingfisher is found in place of it, in a limited area in the southwest. Common from Labrador to Florida, east and west. Winters chiefly in Southern States, and in South America.
Times of Appearance: Migrates north in March; south in December.
For article on habits, food preferences, colors of plumage, description of appearance, how strange nesting habits reveal their ancestry, etc., etc., see page 168 of the Nature Library volume on BIRDS.

Osprey

Parts of Country Where Found: North America from Hudson Bay and Alaska, south to the Equator; nests throughout North America.
Times of Appearance: Migrates north in March; south in October.
For description, means of identification, habits, food preferences, remarkable method of fishing, why it sometimes loses its dinner to the eagle, etc., etc., see page 182 of the Nature Library volume on BIRDS.

MARCH

Phœbe

Parts of Country Where Found: North America from Newfoundland to the South Atlantic States and west to the Rockies. Winters south of the Carolinas, and as far south as Mexico, Central America, and the West Indies.
Times of Appearance: Migrates north in March; south in October. For article on habits, food preferences, why a pair will nest in the same place year after year, kind of nesting place that attracts them, colors of plumage, description of appearance, etc., etc., see page 142 of the Nature Library volume on BIRDS.

Robin

Parts of Country Where Found: North America, from Mexico to Arctic regions.
Times of Appearance: Migrates north in March; south in October or November. Often stays in North through the year.
For article on food preferences, nesting habits, kinds of materials used, how nest differs from most other birds, etc., etc., see page 24 of the Nature Library volume on BIRDS. For color, appearance, and identifying marks, see full-color illustration (frontispiece.)

WILD FLOWERS APPEARING IN MARCH

Adder's Tongue, Yellow; Trout Lily; Dog-Tooth "Violet"

Flowering Season: From March to May.
Where to Look For: Moist open woods and thickets; brooksides.
Parts of Country Where Found: Nova Scotia and Florida to the Mississippi.
For description, manner of growth, etc., etc., see page 17 of Nature Library volume on WILD FLOWERS. For appearance, identifying marks and colors, see full-color illustration facing page 12.

Arbutus, Trailing. Mayflower; Ground Laurel

Flowering Season: From March to May.
Where to Look For: Light sandy loam in woods, especially under evergreen trees, or in mossy, rocky places.
Parts of Country Where Found: Newfoundland to Florida, west to Kentucky and the northwest territory.
For description, manner of growth, etc., etc., see page 157 of Nature Library volume on WILD FLOWERS. For appearance

in form and characteristic color, see full-color illustration facing page 113.

Cabbage, Skunk or Swamp

Flowering Season: From February to April.
Where to Look For: Swamps; wet ground.
Parts of Country Where Found: Nova Scotia and Florida to Minnesota and Iowa.
For appearance, color, description of growing habits, relations with insects, etc., etc., see page 8 of Nature Library volume on WILD FLOWERS.

Hepatica; Liver-leaf; Liverwort

Flowering Season: From December to May. Usually found early in March.
Where to Look For: Woods; light soil on hillsides.
Parts of Country Where Found: Canada to northern Florida, Manitoba to Iowa and Missouri. Most commonly found in eastern parts of this area.
For description, growth, and seeding habits, etc., etc., see page 61 of Nature Library volume on WILD FLOWERS. For appearance in natural surroundings, see full-color illustration facing page 64.

Spring Beauty; Claytonia

Flowering Season: from March to May.
Where to Look For: Moist woods, open groves, low meadows.
Parts of Country Where Found: Nova Scotia to Georgia and Texas; far westward.
For description, growing, and seeding habits, relations with insects, etc., etc., see page 53 of Nature Library volume on WILD FLOWERS.

Saxifrage, Early

Flowering Season: From March to May.
Where to Look For: Rocky woodlands; hillsides.
Parts of Country Where Found: From New Brunswick to Georgia, and westward to beyond the Mississippi.
For growing and seeding habits, relations with insects, description of form and color, why its name means "rock-breaker," etc., etc., see page 90 of Nature Library volume on WILD FLOWERS.

Wake-Robin, Early or Dwarf

Flowering Season: From March to May.
Where to Look For: Rich moist woods and thickets.

MARCH

For description of growing habits, season of leaving, flowering, and seeding, etc., etc., see page 78 of Nature Library volume on TREES. For characteristic shape and color, details of leaf, etc., etc., see full-color illustration facing page 57.

Flowering Dogwood

From March till May one finds the dogwood clothed in white.
For habits of growth, leaving, flowering, seeding, etc., etc., see page 111 of Nature Library volume on TREES. For appearance of tree in flower, details of leaf, seed-vessel, etc., see full-color illustration facing page 101.

Balsam Poplar

When growth starts with the stirring of the sap, the fragrant wax covering the winter buds softens; then the bees collect and store it against a day of need. Whether their homes be hollow trees, or patent hives, weather cracks are carefully sealed up with this waterproof gum, which the bee-keeper knows as "propolis."
For description of appearance and growing habits of tree, season of flowering, leaving, and seeding, details of leaf, etc., etc., see page 79 of Nature Library volume on TREES.

The Starry Magnolia

The Starry Magnolia blooms in March or April, covering itself with star-shaped white flowers.
For appearance of tree and blossoms, habits of growth, kind of country where found, etc., etc., see page 103 of Nature Library volume on TREES.

Weeping Willow

Willows start growth early in spring, putting out their catkins, the two sexes on different trees, before the opening of the leaves. For method by which masculine and feminine trees "marry," description of form and color, habits of growth, leaving, flowering, seeding, etc., etc., see page 83 of Nature Library volume on TREES.

April, The Grass Moon

This month the pioneer bird visitors from the South are joined by a whole troop of newcomers, although the great chorus of feathered songsters will be still incomplete until May. You should get to know them all by sound as well as sight.

In April the robin is even more plentiful, and busy, with his "cheerily, cheerily, cheer-up!" And now you will hear the "purity, purity!" of the "phœbe," and the "quick, quick, quick, quick!" of the flicker in the budding woods. The "I see, I see you," of the meadowlark reaches you from the distant field, and the song sparrow calls his "sweet, sweet, bitter."

To be able to recognize and visualize the wild birds by hearing their songs and other sounds of activity gives the true nature lover rare thrills indeed! April brings the bird student many of these pleasures of recognition, perhaps none finer than the sound that comes to your ear when.

"The partridge beats his throbbing drum."

"There is no bird sound like it," says William Hamilton Gibson, "this soft, murmurous tattoo of the grouse in the bare, freshening woods. It is in harmony with the first heart-throbs and accelerating life of exuberant, awakening Nature—

Partridge "Drumming"

APRIL

the quickening seeds, the flowing sap, the swelling buds.
"Puff! puff! puff! puff! puff! p-r-r-r-r-r-r-r-r!"

Do you know how the partridge does his drumming? There is an interesting controversy about it. Witnesses differ, even after seeing him do it many times.

April offers many thrills to the bird-lover, while to the seeker for wild flowers she brings an ever-increasing number of joys. The early hepatica continues and has been joined in the woodlands by the delicately tinted anemone, or wind-flower, and the pink spring beauty or Claytonia. In the open marshy meadows the cowslip, or marsh marigold, is beginning to appear.

"Dutchman's Breeches"

Along the edges of overhanging rocks the wild columbine is preparing its red, nectar-bearing spurs for the visits of humming birds and big, long-tongued bumblebees. "Dutchman's Breeches" wave upon their delicate stems between the crevices of shaded, moss-grown rocks. Bloodroot, or "Indian Paint," shoots up its single, golden-centred white blossom, offering only a glimpse of fleeting loveliness before it drops its petals and is gone to seed. If it were only for the wild flowers, a walk in the April woods is rich in beauty, but there is more, much more, to see.

The trees are pushing out their first bursts of tender green, and many are in blossom. You may still see the dogwoods, and the less striking blossoms of some of the nut trees are also coming into view. The lengthening and opening bud scales give many varied tints of red, and many leaves are rosy, or lilac tinted, when they first open. Do you know why Nature makes these tree leaves a reddish color for a few days, instead of green?

If, in April, you should chance to see a "mockernut" tree, a member of the hickory tribe, you will always remember it. The long red leaf scales, surrounding each unfolding green shoot, seem like the petals of a great red tulip. And this is only one of the lovely sights that the April woods and fields offer to the person who goes there with his eyes open, and a little knowledge of what to look for.

But you need to know what you are looking for, or you may pass by the most wonderful things without knowing they are there! A boy who has woodchucks in his eye as he crosses a field will be more likely to see one than the boy who is thinking of making a kite. There is no better preparation for seeing a bird, a flower, or a butterfly than to see a good picture of it first. The full-color pictures of the Nature Library will enable you to recognize at a glance the living things you see out of doors.

And what a satisfaction it is, when you have once identified a bird, flower, or tree, to greet its relatives at the next meeting like old friends, and to introduce them to your children or companions of the hike in the open!

In April, Nature is fairly awake for the summer. Every day new growths are springing out, new flowers opening, new bird-songs in the air. Hasten out, on the first Sunday, whether fair or showery, and look for the things that interest you, whether birds, beasts, flowers, or trees. But first be sure you are *prepared* to see them. Read through some of the references in the Nature Library, given below for the month of April, and look at all the pictures. If you do this, you will see more things on your first walk than you ever did on a country stroll before!

APRIL

BIRDS MIGRATING NORTHWARD IN APRIL

Blackbird, Rusty

Parts of Country Where Found: North America, breeding in Alaska, Canada, and the Northeastern States; west in migration to the plains and south to the Gulf.
Times of Appearance: Migrates north in April; south in November.
For description, means of identification, habits, food preferences, surroundings it prefers, etc., etc., see page 122 of Nature Library volume on BIRDS.

Cuckoos, Yellow and Black-billed

Parts of Country Where Found: Southern Canada and United States; rare on Pacific slope; winters in South America.
Times of Appearance: Migrates north in late April; south in September. Summer resident.
For description of appearance, habits, nest, food preferences, why the inside of the bird's stomach looks like a shiny silk hat's surface, etc., etc., see page 171 of Nature Library volume on BIRDS. For color and identifying marks see full-color illustration facing page 159.

Flicker

Parts of Country Where Found: United States, east of Rockies; Alaska and British America, south of Hudson Bay. South in winter to the Gulf Coast and southern Texas.
Times of Appearance: Most commonly seen from April to October.
For article on food preferences, how its tongue is specially adapted to secure one special kind of food, how it "pumps" food into the mouths of its young, nesting habits, etc., etc., see page 157 of Nature Library volume on BIRDS. For color, appearance, and identifying marks, see full-color illustration facing page 158.

Goose, Canada

Parts of Country Where Found: North America at large; nests in British America and northern United States; winters south to Mexico.
Times of Appearance: Chiefly a migrant. Migrations irregular. Goes north in March and April; south in November to December.
For description, means of identification, characteristic formations

of flocks during flight, habits, food preferences etc., etc., see page 235 of Nature Library volume on BIRDS.

Hawk, Night

Parts of Country Where Found: Breeds east of the Plains, from Canada to the northern parts of the Gulf States; winters south to Argentina.
Times of Appearance: Migrates north in late April; south in September and early October.
For article on habits, food preferences, nest, colors of plumage, description of appearance, why superstitious people regard his coming as a bad omen, etc., etc., see page 149 of Nature Library volume on BIRDS.

Heron, Little Green

Parts of Country Where Found: Eastern North America; breeds from southern Canada to the West Indies; winters from the West Indies, southward, rarely in the Southeastern States.
Times of Appearance: Migrates north in April and early May; south in September.
For description, means of identification, habits, food preferences, why they built nests in solitary spots instead of communities, etc., etc., see page 231 of Nature Library volume on BIRDS. For color, appearance, and identifying marks see full-color illustration facing page 223.

Heron, Great Blue

Parts of Country Where Found: North America at large, from Labrador, Hudson Bay, and Alaska; nests locally through range; winters in Southern States, West Indies, Central and South America.
Times of Appearance: Resident in South; summer resident in North. Migrates north in April; south in October or even December.
For article on habits, food preferences, nest, colors of plumage, description of appearance, why this bird is regarded as a low form of bird life in spite of its great size, etc., etc., see page 228 of the Nature Library volume on BIRDS.

Kinglet, Ruby-crowned

Parts of Country Where Found: North America. Breeds from northern United States northward. Winters from southern limit of breeding range to Mexico and Central America.

APRIL

Times of Appearance: North in April; south in October. Rarely a winter resident at the north; most common during migrations. For description, means of identification, habits, food preferences, how his mating song differs from his usual call-note, etc., etc., see page 32 of the Nature Library volume on BIRDS.

Kinglet, Golden-crowned

Parts of Country Where Found: Same as Ruby-crowned.
Times of Appearance: Ditto.
For article on habits, food preferences, nest, colors of plumage, description of appearance, etc., etc., see page 34 of the Nature Library volume on BIRDS.

Martin, Purple

Parts of Country Where Found: Breeds in entire North America except the Pacific Coast region. Winters in Brazil.
Times of Appearance: Migrates north in late April; south in early September.
For description of appearance, habits, nests, food preferences, why "apartment houses" should be put up for them, etc., etc., see page 89 of Nature Library volume on BIRDS. For color and identifying marks see full-color illustration facing page 82.

Meadowlark

Parts of Country Where Found: North America, from Newfoundland to the Gulf and westward to the plains, where the western meadowlark takes its place. Winters from Massachusetts and Illinois southward.
Times of Appearance: Migrates north in March and April; south in October. A few remain north throughout the winter.
For article on habits, food preferences, nest, colors of plumage, why it turns its back while you are watching it, description of appearance, etc., etc., see page 126 of Nature Library volume on BIRDS.

Owl, Short-eared

Parts of Country Where Found: Nearly cosmopolitan; throughout North America, nesting from Virginia northward.
Times of Appearance: Chiefly migratory. Goes north in April; south in November.
For description, means of identification, unusual hunting and nesting habits, food preferences, why it almost never alights on trees, etc., etc., see page 177 of Nature Library volume on BIRDS.

NATURE'S PROGRAM

Rail or Clapp

Parts of Country Where Found: Salt marshes of the Atlantic Coast. Breeds from Connecticut to North Carolina; winters mainly south of New Jersey.
Times of Appearance: Migrates north in April; south in October. A few are winter residents in the north.
For article on habits, food preferences, nest, colors of plumage, peculiar noise made in mating season, description of appearance, etc., etc., see page 226 of Nature Library volume on BIRDS.

Sandpiper, Spotted

Parts of Country Where Found: Breeds throughout North America from the tree limit almost to the Gulf; winters in Southern States and south to Brazil.
Times of Appearance: Migrates north in April; south in September or October.
For description of appearance, means of identification, queer way of "bowing" to spectators, habits, food preferences, etc., etc., see page 217 of Nature Library volume on BIRDS.

Sparrow, Chipping

Parts of Country Where Found: Eastern North America, breeding from Canada to the Southern States; winters chiefly in the Southern States, occasional in the Middle States.
Times of Appearance: Migrates north in April; south in October.
For article on habits, food preferences, special material used to line nest, colors of plumage, description of appearance, etc., etc., see page 109 of Nature Library volume on BIRDS.

Sparrow, Vesper

Parts of Country Where Found: Eastern North America, breeding in southern Canada and the Northern States; winters from the southern of its summer range to the Gulf Coast and middle Texas.
Times of Appearance: Migrates north in April; south in October.
For description, means of identification, habits, exquisite evensong, food preferences, etc., etc., see page 114 of Nature Library volume on BIRDS.

Swallow, Barn

Parts of Country Where Found: Breeds throughout United States. Winters in South and Central America.
Times of Appearance: Migrates north in April; south in September.

APRIL

For article on food preferences, nesting habits, why it plays "crosstag" with its friends at evening, etc., etc., see page 91 of Nature Library volume on BIRDS. For color, appearance, and identifying marks, see full-color illustration facing page 79.

Swallow, Bank

Parts of Country Where Found: Same as Barn Swallow.
Times of Appearance: Migrates north in April; south in September.
For description, means of identification, amazing nesting habits, food preferences, etc., etc., see page 94 of Nature Library volume on BIRDS.

Swallow, Tree

Parts of Country Where Found: Breeds from northern North America to southern California, Missouri, and Virginia; winters from the Southern States to Central America.
Times of Appearance: Migrates north in April and May; south in September and October.
For description of appearance, habits, nest, why they often rear two broods in a season, food preferences, etc., etc., see page 94 of Nature Library volume on BIRDS. For color and identifying marks, see full-color illustration facing page 83.

Swift, Chimney

Parts of Country Where Found: Breeds east of the plains, from Canada to the Gulf Coast; winters south of the United States.
Times of Appearance: Migrates north in April; south in September and October.
For description, means of identification, habits, food preferences, why it looks like a bat in flight, etc., etc., see page 151 of the Nature Library volume on BIRDS.

Tanager, Summer

Parts of Country Where Found: Most common in Southern States; rare north of Pennsylvania. Eastern States. Winters in tropics.
Times of Appearance: Appears in Southern States from April and October. Irregular migrant north of the Carolinas.
For article on habits, food preferences, nest, colors of plumage, description of appearance, etc., etc., see page 85 of Nature Library volume on BIRDS.

Thrasher, Brown

Parts of Country Where Found: United States east of the Rockies. Nests from the Gulf States to Manitoba and Montreal. Winters south of Virginia.

Times of Appearance: Migrates into Northern States in late April. Goes south in October.

For description of appearance, habits, nest, food preferences, why he chooses a conspicuous perch when about to give his remarkable song, etc., etc., see page 47 of Nature Library volume on BIRDS. For color and identifying marks see full-color illustration facing page 50.

Towhee

Parts of Country Where Found: From Labrador to the Southern States, west to the Rockies; farther south in winter.

Times of Appearance: Migrates north in April; south in September and October. Rarely a winter resident at the north.

For description, means of identification, habits, food preferences, why it is sometimes called the "Ground Robin," etc., etc., see page 102 of Nature Library volume on BIRDS. For color, appearance, and identifying marks see full-color illustration facing page 99.

Vireo, Red-eyed

Parts of Country Where Found: United States to Rockies and northward. Winters in South America.

Times of Appearance: Migrates north in April; south in October.

For article on habits, food preferences, remarkable nest, colors of plumage, description of appearance, why the vireo is called "the preacher" etc., etc., see page 72 of Nature Library volume on BIRDS.

Vireo, White-eyed

Parts of Country Where Found: Breeds in eastern United States as far north as Massachusetts or rarely Vermont; winters from South Carolina to Central America.

Times of Appearance: Migrates north in April; south in late September and October.

For description, means of identification, habits, food preferences, use of "cuss words," custom of hatching the egg of another kind of bird, etc., see page 74 of the Nature Library volume on BIRDS.

Warbler, Myrtle

Parts of Country Where Found: Eastern North America; occasional on Pacific slope. Summers from Minnesota and northern

APRIL

New England north to fur countries. Winters from Middle States south to Central America; a few remain at northern United States all winter.
Times of Appearance: Migrates north in April; south in October and November.
For article on habits, food preferences, nest, colors of plumage, description of appearance, why it is called "myrtle," etc., etc., see page 64 of Nature Library volume on "BIRDS

Warbler, Black and White Creeping

Parts of Country Where Found: Eastern United States and west to the plains; north as far as the fur countries. Winters in tropics south of Florida.
Times of Appearance: Migrates north in April; south in late September. Summer resident.
For description, means of identification, why it is often mistaken for another bird, habits, food preferences, etc., etc., see page 69 of Nature Library volume on BIRDS.

Whippoorwill

Parts of Country Where found: Eastern North America, east of the plains, from southern Canada to the Gulf. Winters from the Southern States to northern South America.
Times of Appearance: Migrates north in late April; south in September and early October.
For article on food preferences, why most people have heard it but few ever see it, why it builds no nest, etc., etc., see page 147 of Nature Library volume on BIRDS. For color, appearance, and identifying marks see full-color illustration facing page 143.

Woodpecker, Yellow-bellied

Parts of Country Where Found: Eastern North America. Breeds from Labrador to the Northern States. Winters in the Middle and Southern States.
Times of Appearance: Migrates north in April; south in October.
For article on habits, food preferences, why he apparently gets "drunk" and is called the "sapsucker," nest, colors of plumage, description of appearance, etc., etc., see page 162 of Nature Library volume on BIRDS.

Wren, House

Parts of Country Where Found: North America, from Manitoba to the Gulf. Most common in the United States, from the Mississippi eastward. Winters south of the Carolinas.

Times of Appearance: In north, April. In south, October. Common summer resident.

For description of appearance, habits, nest, food preferences, why the male begins to build a nest before he finds a mate, etc., etc., see page 44 of Nature Library volume on BIRDS and for color and identifying marks see full-color illustration facing page 47.

WILD FLOWERS APPEARING IN APRIL

Anemone, Wood; or Wind-flower

Flowering Season: From April to June.
Where to Look For: Woodlands, hillsides, light soil, partial shade.
Parts of Country Where Found: Canada and United States, south to Georgia, west to Rockies.

For description: growing and seeding habits, interesting legends about it, relations with insects, etc., etc., see page 63 of Nature Library volume on WILD FLOWERS.

Adder's Tongue, Yellow (See March)

Baneberry, White; Cohosh

Flowering Season: April to June.
Where to Look For: Cool, shady, moist woods.
Parts of Country Where Found: Nova Scotia and Georgia to far West.

For description of characteristics—form, color, flowering, and seeding habits, why the berries are called "doll's eyes," etc., etc., see page 73 of Nature Library volume on WILD FLOWERS.

Bloodroot; Indian Paint

Flowering Season: April and May.
Where to Look For: Rich woods and their borders, low hillsides.
Parts of Country Where Found: Nova Scotia to Florida, west to Nebraska.

For growing and seeding habits, relations with insects, description of form and color, why it was called "Indian Paint," etc., etc., see page 76 of Nature Library volume on WILD FLOWERS.

Arbutus, Trailing (See March)

APRIL

Bluets; Quaker Ladies or Bonnets

Flowering Season: From April to July, or sparsely through summer.
Where to Look For: Moist meadows, wet rocks and banks.
Parts of Country Where Found: Eastern Canada and United States, west to Michigan, south to Georgia and Alabama.
For description, growing and seeding habits, relations with insects, why one of its names is "Houstonia," etc., etc., see page 216 of Nature Library volume on WILD FLOWERS.

Betony, Wood; Lousewort; Beefsteak Plant

Flowering Season: From April to June.
Where to Look For: Dry, open woods and thickets.
Parts of Country Where Found: Nova Scotia and Florida to Manitoba, Colorado and Kansas.
For growing and seeding habits, relations with insects, description of form and color, interesting superstitions connected with the plant, etc., etc., see page 211 of Nature Library volume on WILD FLOWERS.

Brooklime, American

Flowering Season: From April to September.
Where to Look For: In brooks, ponds, ditches, swamps.
Parts of Country Where Found: From coast to coast, Alaska and Quebec to California, New Mexico, and Pennsylvania.
For description of characteristics—form, color, flowering and seeding habits, relations with insects, pleasing sentiments connected with it, etc.—see page 205 of Nature Library volume on WILD FLOWERS.

Buttercup, Swamp or Marsh

Flowering Season: From April to July.
Where to Look For: Low, rich meadows.
Parts of Country Where Found: Georgia and Kentucky, far northward.
For description, growing and seeding habits, relations with insects, etc., etc., see page 59 of Nature Library volume on WILD FLOWERS.

Buttercup, Tufted

Flowering Season: April and May.
Where to Look For: Woods and rocky hillsides.
Parts of Country Where Found: Texas and Manitoba to the Atlantic.

NATURE'S PROGRAM

For growing and seeding habits, relations with insects, description of form and color, etc., etc., see page 58 of Nature Library volume on WILD FLOWERS.

Cabbage, Skunk or Swamp (See March)

Carrion-flower

Flowering Season: From April to June.
Where to Look For: Moist soil, thickets, woods and roadside fences.
Parts of Country Where Found: Northern Canada to the Gulf States, west to Nebraska.
For description, growing and seeding habits, relations with insects, why it has such a repellent odor, why bees do not visit it, etc., etc., see page 25 of Nature Library volume on WILD FLOWERS.

Dogwood, Flowering

Flowering Season: From April to June.
Where to Look For: Woodlands, rocky thickets, wooded roadsides.
Parts of Country Where Found: Maine and Florida to Ontario and Texas.
For article on growing and seeding habits, relations with insects, description of form and color, why farmers watch for it at corn-planting time, etc., etc., see page 143 of Nature Library volume on WILD FLOWERS.

Dutchman's Breeches

Flowering Season: April and May.
Where to Look For: Rich, rocky woods.
Parts of Country Where Found: Nova Scotia to the Carolinas, west to Nebraska.
For description, growth, and seeding habits, etc., etc., see page 79 of Nature Library volume on WILD FLOWERS. For appearance in natural surroundings, see full-color illustration facing page 76.

Celandine, Greater; Swallow-wort

Flowering Season: April to September.
Where to Look For: Dry wasteland, fields, roadsides, gardens, near dwellings.
Parts of Country Where Found: Naturalized from Europe in eastern United States.
For appearance, color, description of growing habits, relations with

APRIL

insects, quaint superstitions connected with the plant, etc., etc., see page 78 of Nature Library volume on WILD FLOWERS.

Clover, Common Red

Flowering Season: April to November.
Where to Look For: Fields, meadows, roadsides.
Parts of Country Where Found: Common throughout Canada and United States.
For description, growing and seeding habits, relations with insects, why a dream about clover is thought to mean good fortune, etc., etc., see page 107 of Nature Library volume on WILD FLOWERS.

Columbine, Wild

Flowering Season: From April to July.
Where to Look For: Rocky places, rich woodlands.
Parts of Country Where Found: Nova Scotia to the Northwest territory and the Rockies, south to the Gulf States.
For description, manner of growth, why it is a favorite "lunch-counter" for the humming bird, etc., etc., see page 68 of Nature Library volume on WILD FLOWERS. For appearance, identifying marks and colors, see full-color illustration (frontispiece).

Five-finger; Common Cinquefoil

Flowering Season: From April to August.
Where to Look For: Dry fields, roadsides, hills, banks.
Parts of Country Where Found: Quebec to Georgia, and west beyond the Mississippi.
For growing and seeding habits, relations with insects, description of form and color, former use in medicine during Middle Ages, etc., etc., see page 98 of Nature Library volume on WILD FLOWERS.

Geranium, Wild or Spotted; Crane's-Bill

Flowering Season: From April to July.
Where to Look For: Open woods, thickets, shady roadsides.
Parts of Country Where Found: Newfoundland and Georgia, to beyond the Mississippi.
For description of characteristics—form, color, flowering and seeding habits, relations with insects, interesting story of discoveries made on this plant by early botanists, etc., etc., see page 118 of Nature Library volume on WILD FLOWERS.

Hepatica (See March)
Honeysuckle, Wild; Pink, Purple, or Wild Azalea
Flowering Season: April and May.
Where to Look For: Moist rocky woods, or dry woods and thickets.
Parts of Country Where Found: Maine and Illinois to the Gulf.
For description, growing and seeding habits, relations with insects, story of its export to Europe and development by florists there, etc., etc., see page 150 of Nature Library volume on WILD FLOWERS.

Jack-in-the-Pulpit
Flowering Season: April to June.
Where to Look For: Moist woodland and thickets.
Parts of Country Where Found: Nova Scotia and Minnesota, south to the Gulf States.
For description, growth, and seeding habits, why he is really a cruel murderer instead of a pious preacher, etc., etc., see page 5 of Nature Library volume on WILD FLOWERS. For appearance in natural surroundings, see full-color illustration facing page 5.

Marigold, Marsh; American Cowslip
Flowering Season: From April to June.
Where to Look For: Springy ground, low meadows, swamps, ditches, river banks.
Parts of Country Where Found: Carolina to Iowa and the Rockies, and very far north.
For description, manner of growth, how it was named for the Virgin Mary, etc., etc., see page 66 of Nature Library volume on WILD FLOWERS. For appearance, identifying marks and colors, see full-color illustration facing page 161.

Meadow-rue, Early
Flowering Season: April and May.
Where to Look For: Open, rocky woods.
Parts of Country Where Found: Alabama to Labrador, and west to Missouri.
For appearance, color, description of growing habits, etc., etc., see page 60 of Nature Library volume on WILD FLOWERS.

Orchis, Showy or Gay
Flowering Season: April to June.
Where to Look For: Rich, moist woods, especially under hemlocks.

APRIL

Parts of Country Where Found: New Brunswick and Ontario to the Southern States; westward to Nebraska.
For description of characteristics—form, color, flowering and seeding habits, relations with insects, remarkable mechanical devices for their use, etc., etc., see page 35 of Nature Library volume on WILD FLOWERS.

Pink, Wild; Catchfly

Flowering Season: April to June.
Where to Look For: Dry, gravelly, sandy, or rocky soil.
Parts of Country Where Found: New England, south to Georgia, west to Kentucky.
For growing and seeding habits, how nectar is protected for use of butterflies only, description of form and color, etc., etc., see page 51 of Nature Library volume on WILD FLOWERS.

Pink, Ground or Moss

Flowering Season: April to June.
Where to Look For: Rocky ground, hillsides.
Parts of Country Where Found: Southern New York and Florida to Kentucky and Michigan.
For description, manner of growth, etc., etc., see page 181 of Nature Library volume on WILD FLOWERS. For appearance in form and characteristic color, see full-color illustration facing page 145.

Partridge Vine, Twin-berry

Flowering Season: From April to June, sometimes again in fall.
Where to Look For: Woods; usually, but not always dry ones.
Parts of Country Where Found: Nova Scotia and the Gulf States to Minnesota and Texas.
For appearance, color, description of growing habits, relations with birds, etc., etc., see page 214 of Nature Library volume on WILD FLOWERS.

Plantain, Robin's or Poor Robin's, or Robert's Blue Spring Daisy; Daisy-leaved Fleabane

Flowering Season: April to June.
Where to Look For: Moist ground, hills, banks, grassy fields.
Parts of Country Where Found: United States and Canada, east of the Mississippi.
For description of characteristics—form, color, flowering and seeding habits, etc., etc., see page 237 of Nature Library volume on WILD FLOWERS.

Pond Lily, Large Yellow; Water Lily

Flowering Season: From April to September.
Where to Look For: Standing water, ponds, slow streams.
Parts of Country Where Found: Nova Scotia and the Gulf to the Rockies.
For description, manner of growth, etc., etc., see page 54 of Nature Library volume on WILD FLOWERS. For appearance, identifying marks and colors, see full-color illustration facing page 48.

Solomon's Seal, Hairy, or True

Flowering Season: From April to June.
Where to Look For: Woods, thickets, shady banks.
Parts of Country Where Found: New Brunswick to Florida, west to Michigan.
For appearance, color, description of growing habits, how to tell the age of the plant by its root, how it was named, etc., etc., see page 20 of Nature Library volume on WILD FLOWERS.

Shooting Star; American Cowslip

Flowering Season: From April to May.
Where to Look For: Prairies, open woods, moist cliffs.
Parts of Country Where Found: Pennsylvania, southward and westward; Texas to Manitoba.
For growing and seeding habits, relations with insects, description of form and color, etc., etc., see page 163 of Nature Library volume on WILD FLOWERS.

Spring Beauty (See March)

Saxifrage, Early (See March)

Trillium, Purple; Ill-scented Wake-Robin

Flowering Season: From April to June.
Where to Look For: Rich, moist woods.
Parts of Country Where Found: Nova Scotia and Manitoba to North Carolina and Missouri.
For description, growing and seeding habits, relations with insects, why it has such a repellent odor, etc., etc., see page 23 of Nature Library volume on WILD FLOWERS.

White Violets, Lance and Primrose-leaved, and Sweet White

Flowering Season: From April to June.
Where to Look For: Moist meadows; damp, mossy places; borders of streams.

APRIL

Parts of Country Where Found: United States and southern Canada.
For appearance, color, description of growing habits, relations with insects, etc., etc., see page 135 of Nature Library volume on WILD FLOWERS.

Violets, Downy and Smooth Yellow

Flowering Season: Downy, from April to May. Smooth, earlier.
Where to Look For: Dry woods.
Parts of Country Where Found: Nova Scotia to Manitoba and southward.
For description, growing and seeding habits, relations with insects, etc., etc., see page 134 of Nature Library volume on WILD FLOWERS.

Wake-Robin, Nodding

Flowering Season: April to June.
Where to Look For: Same places as other trilliums.
Parts of Country Where Found: Newfoundland and Manitoba to Pennsylvania and Michigan.
For growing and seeding habits, description of form and color, etc., etc., see page 22 of Nature Library volume on WILD FLOWERS.

Wake-Robin, Sessile-flowered

Flowering Season: April and May.
Where to Look For: Deep, rich moist woods and thickets.
Parts of Country Where Found: Pennsylvania and Minnesota, nearly to the Gulf.
For description of characteristics, form, color, flowering habits, relations with insects, etc., etc., see page 24 of Nature Library volume on WILD FLOWERS.

Wake-Robin, Early or Dwarf (See March)

BUTTERFLIES TO BE WATCHED FOR IN APRIL

Cabbage Butterfly, White or Imported

Found practically wherever cabbages are grown. In the Northern States the insect passes through the winter within the chrysalis, coming forth rather early in spring.
For description of characteristic life changes, parts of country

where found, habits of wintering, etc., etc., see page 83 of Nature Library volume on BUTTERFLIES.

Dusky-wing, Persius's

The butterfly is found from ocean to ocean along the northern tier of states. It also occurs in the Eastern States as far south as Florida, as well as in the states along the Pacific Coast.
Caterpillars remain unchanged until April or May when they transform into chrysalids to emerge in May as butterflies.
For favorite food plants, habits of wintering, description of life changes (caterpillar, chrysalid, and mature form), number of broods produced each season, etc., etc., see page 276 of Nature Library volume on BUTTERFLIES.

Hop Merchant or Comma

They may often be seen sunning themselves on bright days in April and May. The eggs are likely to be laid late in May or even early in June. Has a very wide range, being found from New England to Texas and from the Northwestern States to the Carolinas.
For description of life changes, habits of wintering, number of broods produced each season, parts of country where found, favorite food plants, etc., etc., see page 153 of Nature Library volume on BUTTERFLIES. For appearance in natural surroundings, characteristic markings, etc., etc., see full-color illustration facing page 161.

Sooty Wing

This species is widely distributed, occurring over practically the whole of the United States, except in the states along the Canadian border from Wisconsin west. The butterfly comes forth in April or May.
For favorite food plants, habits of wintering, description of life changes, number of broods produced each season, etc., etc., see page 277 of Nature Library volume on BUTTERFLIES.

Zebra Swallowtail

Marcellus—the early spring form. Telamonides—the late spring form. Ajax—the summer form.
Southern butterfly, found as far west as Texas and the Rocky Mountains and having its northern limits in a zone ranging approximately from Massachusetts to Nebraska.
For description of life changes, habits of wintering, number of

APRIL

broods produced each season, parts of country where found, favorite food plants, etc., etc., see page 76 of Nature Library volume on BUTTERFLIES. For appearance in natural surroundings, chraacteristic markings, etc., etc., see full-color illustration facing page 80.

TREES TO BE NOTICED IN APRIL

The Redbud

The unusual color leads to a very general recognition of this tree among people who go into the April woods for early violets.
For appearance of tree and blossoms, habits of growth, kind of country where found, etc., etc., see page 182 of Nature Library volume on TREES.

The Sheepberry

The fragrant white flowers light up the tree from April to June with their flat clusters three to five inches across.
For description of appearance and growing habits of tree, season of flowering, leaving and seeding, details of leaf, etc., etc., see page 114 of Nature Library volume on TREES.

The Palo Verde Acacia

Clustered flowers, like little yellow roses, cover the branches in April.
For appearance of tree and blossoms, habits of growth, kind of country where found, etc., etc., see page 190 of Nature Library volume on TREES.

May, The Planting Moon

In May the spirit of spring reaches its high tide. Even the hardwood trees, the oaks and ashes, are at last leaved out and blossoming.

The other trees are often masses of fresh green before the ash finally awakes. Not until May do the rusty yellow winter buds of the white ash swell and throw out their leaves and flowers. Some of these trees are masculine; others feminine. One bears flowers with "stamens"; another with "pistils." Do you know how the marriage of the ash trees takes place?

If you see a small white pine in the woods this month, notice how the new season's growth is starting, fresh green, at the tip-top bud of the little tree. Round its base are five clustered green buds, forming a circle. Tie a marking string around the terminal bud, and, in the fall, come back and look at this same tree again. The end bud will then be several inches long. The five clustered buds will be five slender twigs. All, including the terminal bud, will be surrounded, in turn, by new circles of five green buds. Do you know how to use this knowledge in telling, at a glance, the age of any pine tree you see?

Terminal Buds of Pine

The trees in May offer many lovely sights to the hiker, but none finer than the horse-chestnut in bloom. The upturning branches, like the arms of candelabra, are each tipped with a white blossom cluster pointed like a candle flame.

The red oak is another tree with very abundant and conspicuous blossoms, usually opening when the leaves are half-grown in May. Beautiful, fringe-like, pollen-bearing strings droop from the twigs in clusters.

These are only a few of the interesting leaves and blossoms that await your walk in the May woods.

Now that the majority of field flowers are coming into blossom, you have an opportunity to begin some very interesting detective work, for in May there are also a great many different kinds of butterflies on the wing.

Horse-chestnut Blooms

Try to find out by repeated observations which butterflies are attracted to certain flowers. Take the Nature Library volume on Butterflies, and become familiar with the appearance of the "Red Admiral." Then notice, in the fields, how frequently you see this beautiful variety perched upon the blossoms and leaves of the common nettle. What is it doing there? Why is it called "the nettle butterfly"?

The "Nettle Butterfly"

You know how common the thistle is. Every fence corner and roadside is decorated with this prickly, highly successful plant. Wait beside it for a while on your May walk, and it is more than likely that you will see a "Painted Lady" butterfly alight upon it. Why is the "Painted Lady" always found wherever thistles are growing? To find out the relationships between fifty wild flowers and the particular insects which visit them would be a summer's detective work of which any nature lover might be proud, and which would yield priceless results in the training of the eye and mind in observation. They need to be exercised and trained together, and the Nature Library is adapted to help, no matter what department of Nature interests you most.

Even without taking the insect visitors into account, many of the flowers hold cunning mysteries in store for the observer who comes armed with a little knowledge of their ways.

If you stroll through the moist May woods you will perhaps come upon little mauve-winged blooms among the mosses, fluttering in the breeze like a brood of tiny purple butterflies with fringy tails. This is the "false wintergreen" or "fringed polygala." It is so pretty that you are tempted to pick it, and would do so, except that you think this would prevent the spreading of its seed for next year's growth of similar flowers. But you can pick and carry away a whole bouquet of this flower without interfering to any great extent with its spreading of seed. How? That is the polygala's secret. Dig the plant out by the roots and you will find that it has also a crop of underground flowers which can and do produce seeds all by themselves!

Here is another plant that holds its secret fast until the coming of the bearer of true flower knowledge.

Fringed Polygala

Painted Cup

# MAY

Perhaps you have seen it blossoming, flooding low meadows of May with "meadow fire," as it is sometimes called.

> "Scarlet tufts
> Are glowing in the green, like flakes of fire!
> The wanderers of the prairie know them well,
> And call that brilliant flower the 'painted cup!'"

And yet the brilliant part of this plant, the part of which Bryant thus sings, is not the flower at all! The actual flower of the "painted cup" is an insignificant little green thing which no one would notice unless it was pointed out. So the Nature Library volume on Wild Flowers will enable you to answer the question, "When is a flower not a flower?" and to find out many other fascinating mysteries that you would miss knowing without its aid.

May is so rich in the beauty and interest of its flowers, birds, trees, and living creatures that we can only pick out a few notes of the great symphony Nature is playing. Pick out the subjects you fancy from the following lists and "read up" before you start out for your next walk.

BIRDS MIGRATING NORTHWARD IN MAY

Bittern

Parts of Country Where Found: Temperate North America; nests usually north of Virginia; winters from that state south to the West Indies.
Times of Appearance: Migrates north in May; south in October. For description, means of identification, habits, nest, food preferences, etc., see page 232 of the Nature Library volume on BIRDS.

Bobolink

Parts of Country Where Found: North America, from Eastern coast to Western prairies. Migrates in early autumn to Southern States, and in winter to South America and West Indies.
Times of Appearance: Migrates northward in early May; southward July to October.

For description of appearance, habits, nest, food preferences, etc., see page 130 of the Nature Library volume on BIRDS. For color and identifying marks see full-color illustration facing page 134.

Bunting, Indigo

Parts of Country Where Found: North America from Hudson Bay to Panama. Most common in eastern U. S. Winters in Central America and Mexico.
Times of Appearance: Migrates north in May; south in September.
For article on food preferences, nesting habits, appearance, etc., see page 98 of the Nature Library volume on BIRDS.

Catbird

Parts of Country Where Found: British America to Mexico; west to Rockies, rarely to Pacific Coast. Winters in Southern States, Central America, and Cuba.
Times of Appearance: Migrates north in May; south in November.
For article on food preferences, song, nesting habits, etc., see page 49 of Nature Library volume on BIRDS. For color, appearance, and identifying marks see full-color illustration facing page 51.

Chat, Yellow-breasted

Parts of Country Where Found: North America, from Ontario to Central America and west to the plains. Most common in Middle Atlantic States.
Times of Appearance: Migrates northward in early May; southward late August and September.
For description, nesting habits, food preferences, song and call, etc., see page 57 of the Nature Library volume on BIRDS.

Chickadee

Parts of Country Where Found: Eastern North America. North of the Carolinas to Labrador.
Times of Appearance: Permanent resident in northern parts of the U. S. A few migrate north in May; southward in late September.
For article on habits, food preferences, etc., see page 34 of the Nature Library volume on BIRDS. For color, appearance, and identifying marks see full-color illustration facing page 38.

MAY

Coot

Parts of Country Where Found: North America at large, from Greenland and Alaska to West Indies and Central America; nests throughout range, but more rarely on Atlantic Coast.
Times of Appearance: Resident in the south. In north is chiefly a spring and autumn migrant; northward April and May, southward September to November.
For appearance, identifying marks, plumage, nest, food, etc., see Nature Library volume on BIRDS, page 226.

Duck, Pintail

Parts of Country Where Found: North America at large, nesting north of Illinois to the Arctic Ocean; winters from central U. S. southward to Panama and West Indies.
Times of Appearance: Winter resident in south; chiefly a spring and autumn migrant, or more rarely a winter visitor, in the northern U. S.
For description of habits, nest, food preferences, etc., see page 242 of the Nature Library volume on BIRDS. For plumage, appearance, and identifying marks see full-color illustration facing page 227.

Duck, Shoveler

Parts of Country Where Found: Northern Hemisphere; in America more common in the interior; breeds regularly from Minnesota north, and in scattered locations as far south as Texas, but not in the Atlantic States; winters from southern Illinois and Virginia south to northern South America.
Times of Appearance: Winter visitor in the south; spring and autumn migrant north of Washington, D. C., more abundant in autumn migrations in the East.
For article on food preferences, nesting habits, etc., see Nature Library volume on BIRDS, page 239. For color, appearance, and identifying marks, see full-color illustration opposite page 226.

Flycatcher, Crested

Parts of Country Where Found: Breeds in eastern North America from southern Canada to the Gulf; winters in Mexico and Central America.
Times of Appearance: Migrates north in May, south in September.
For identifying marks, colors, nesting habits, food, song and call, etc., see page 141 of the Nature Library volume on BIRDS.

Flycatcher, Least

Parts of Country Where Found: Breeds in Canada and northern U. S. east of the Rockies; winters from Mexico to Peru.

Goldfinch

Parts of Country Where Found: North America, breeding from lower Canada to (but not including) the southern tier of states; winters over most of summer area and south to the Gulf Coast.
Times of Appearance: Migrates north in May; south in October. Common summer resident in north; frequent throughout winter as well.
For full-page color illustration, with article describing habits, nest, food preferences, song, etc., see page 115 of Nature Library volume on BIRDS.

Grosbeak, Rose-breasted

Parts of Country Where Found: Eastern North America, from southern Canada to central Kansas and New Jersey, and farther south in mountains; winters from southern Mexico to Ecuador.
Times of Appearance: Migrates north early May; south in September.
For article describing color of plumage and identifying marks, habits, nest, food, call and song, etc., see page 100 of Nature Library volume on BIRDS.

Humming-bird, Ruby-throated

Parts of Country Where Found: Summers in eastern North America, from northern Canada to the Gulf. Winters in Central America.
Times of Appearance: Migrates northward in May; southward in October.
For description, means of identification, habits, nest building, food preferences, etc., see page 153 of Nature Library volume on BIRDS. For full-color illustration, see page 150.

Kingbird

Parts of Country Where Found: North America east of the Rockies, breeding from southern Canada almost to the Gulf. Winters from southern Mexico to Bolivia.
Times of Appearance: Migrates north in May; south in September.
For means of identification, plumage, nesting habits, food, song, etc., see page 139 of Nature Library volume on BIRDS.

MAY

Oriole, Baltimore

Parts of Country Where Found: Lower Canada, and the whole U. S. east of the Rockies. Winters from Southern Mexico to Central America. Most common in the Eastern States below 55° north latitude.
Times of Appearance: Migrates north early May; southward in September.
For article describing this bird, means of identification, nest building, food, calls, song, etc., see page 123 of Nature Library volume on BIRDS. Full-color illustration facing page 130.

Oriole, Orchard

Parts of Country Where Found: Breeds in eastern U. S., but rarely in the northern tier of states; winters from Mexico to Central America.
Times of Appearance: Migrates north early May; south late August and September.
For article giving appearance and identifying marks, nesting habits, food preferences, etc., see page 124 of Nature Library volume on BIRDS.

Oven-bird

Parts of Country Where Found: Northern U. S. to the Rockies; winters from southernmost states to Central America.
Times of Appearance: Migrates northward in May; southward in October. Common summer resident.
For description, means of identification, nesting habits, food, song, etc., see page 60 of Nature Library volume on BIRDS.

Pewee, Wood

Parts of Country Where Found: Breeds from Manitoba and Prince Edward Island to eastern Nebraska and the Gulf; winters from Nicaragua to Peru.
Times of Appearance: Migrates north in May; southward in September.
For article describing color of plumage and other means of identification, nesting habits, song, food preferences, etc., see page 144 of Nature Library volume on BIRDS.

Plover, Semipalmated or Ring-necked

Parts of Country Where Found: Breeds in British America; winters from southern Lower California and South Carolina to Patagonia,

Chile and the Galapagos. Occasionally seen in Siberia and Greenland.
Times of Appearance: Migrates northward in May; southward in August and September. In northern U. S. transient only.
For description, means of identification, food preferences, nesting habits, etc., see page 215 of Nature Library volume on BIRDS.

Rail, Carolina or Sora

Parts of Country Where Found: Temperate North America; more abundant on the Atlantic than on the Pacific slope. Nests from Kansas, Illinois, and New York north to Hudson Bay; winters from Southern States to West Indies and northern South America.
Times of Appearance: Migrates north April and May; south August to October.
For article describing habits, food preferences, nest, call, etc., see page 224 of Nature Library volume on BIRDS. Full-color illustration facing page 215.

Redstart

Parts of Country Where Found: North America to upper Canada. West occasionally, as far as the Pacific Coast, but commonly found in summer in the Atlantic and Middle States.
Times of Appearance: Migrates north in early May; south at end of September. Summer resident.
For article descriptive of this bird, plumage, nest, habits, food preferences, song and call, etc., see page 55 of Nature Library volume on BIRDS. Full-color illustration faces page 67, showing color, identifying marks, etc.

Sandpiper, Least

Parts of Country Where Found: Range like that of semipalmated plover; but seen occasionally also in Europe.
Times of Appearance: Migrates north in May; south August to October. Transient only in northern U. S.
For descriptive article, giving color of plumage and other means of identification, nesting habits, food preferences, etc., see page 216 of Nature Library volume on BIRDS.

Shrike, Loggerhead

Parts of Country Where Found: Eastern U. S. to the plains.
Times of Appearance: Migrates north in May; south in October.

MAY

For description, means of identification, preferred foods, nesting habits, etc., see page 77 of Nature Library volume on BIRDS.

Sparrow, White-crowned

Parts of Country Where Found: Breeds from the northern limit of trees southward to central Quebec in the east, and in the west as far south as central California and Wyoming; winters in the southwest. Rare in the East.
Times of Appearance: Migrates north in May, southward in October.
For article describing color of plumage, marks of identification, nesting, food, etc., see page 112 of Nature Library volume on BIRDS.

Tanager, Scarlet

Parts of Country Where Found: North America from northern Canada boundaries to Kansas, northern Georgia, and the mountains of South Carolina. Winters in South America.
Times of Appearance: Migrates northward in May; southward in October.
For descriptive article, giving marks of identification, color of plumage, food preferences, nest, song, etc., see page 83 of Nature Library volume on BIRDS. Full-color illustration faces page 78.

Veery

Parts of Country Where Found: Breeds from northern Michigan and Newfoundland to northern Illinois and northern New Jersey, and in the Alleghanies as far south as northern Georgia; winters in northern South America.
Times of Appearance: Migrates north in May; south in October. Article describing appearance, food preferences, nesting habits, song and calls, etc., will be found on page 30 of Nature Library volume on BIRDS. Full-color illustration, giving marks of identification, color of plumage, etc., faces page 35.

Vireo, Warbling

Parts of Country Where Found: Breeds from Manitoba to northwestern Texas and to Virginia; winters south of the U. S.
Times of Appearance: Migrates north in May; southward in September.
Descriptive article, giving means of identification, nesting habits, food preferences, song, etc., will be found on page 76 of Nature Library volume on BIRDS.

Warbler, Blackburnian

Parts of Country Where Found: Eastern North America, breeding from Manitoba to Minn. and Conn., and farther south in mountains. Winters in South America.
Times of Appearance: Migrates north in May; south in September.
For plumage, identifying marks, nesting habits, food preferences, song and calls, etc., see article on page 62 of Nature Library volume on BIRDS.

Warbler, Chestnut-sided

Parts of Country Where Found: Eastern North America, breeding from Manitoba and Labrador to New Jersey and Illinois; farther south in the Alleghanies. Winters in the tropics.
Times of Appearance: Migrates northward in May; southward in September.
For article on appearance, habits, food preferences, nest, song, etc., see page 63 of Nature Library volume on BIRDS. Full-color illustration, showing plumage and other identifying marks, to be found facing page 70.

Warbler, Yellow

Parts of Country Where Found: North America, except the Southwest. Nests from Gulf States to fur countries; winters south from Gulf States to northern South America.
Times of Appearance: Migrates northward in May; southward in September.
Descriptive article, giving marks of identification, plumage, nesting habits, food preferences, song, etc., to be found on page 65 of Nature Library volume on BIRDS.

Wren, Marsh

Parts of Country Where Found: Breeds in southern British America and the Northern States; winters in southern U. S.
Times of Appearance: Migrates north in May; south in September.
For appearance, marks of identification, nesting habits, food preferences, etc., see page 42 of Nature Library volume on BIRDS.

Yellow-throat, Maryland

Parts of Country Where Found: Eastern North America, west to the plains; most common east of the Alleghanies. Nests from the Gulf States to Labrador and Manitoba; winters south of Gulf States to Panama.

MAY

Times of Appearance: Migrates northward in May; southward in September.
Descriptive article, giving means of identification, plumage, nesting habits, song and calls, food, etc., to be found on page 58 of Nature Library volume on BIRDS.

WILD FLOWERS APPEARING IN MAY

Adder's Tongue, Yellow; Trout Lily; Dog-tooth Violet (See March)

Anemone, Wood (See April)

Arbutus, Trailing; Mayflower; Ground Laurel (See March)

Arethusa; Indian Pink

Flowering Season: From May to June
Parts of Country Where Found: North Carolina and Indiana north to the fur countries.
Where to Look For: Northern bogs and swamps.
For description, manner of growth, etc., see page 42 of Nature Library volume on WILD FLOWERS. For appearance, identifying marks and colors, see full-color illustration facing page 32.

Baneberry (See April)

Barberry; Pepperidge-bush

Flowering Season: May and June
Parts of Country Where Found: Native to Europe and Asia; naturalized in New England and Middle States; less common in Canada and the West.
Where to Look For: Thickets, roadsides, dry or gravelly soil.
For description, growth and seeding habits, etc., see page 75 of Nature Library volume on WILD FLOWERS.

Bloodroot (See April)
Bluets (See April)

Beard-tongue, Hairy

Flowering Season: May to July
Parts of Country Where Found: Ontario to Florida, Manitoba to Texas.
Where to Look For: Dry or rocky fields, thickets, and open woods.
For appearance, color, manner of growth and seeding, relations with insects, etc., see page 200 of Nature Library volume on WILD FLOWERS.

Bellflower, Clasping; Venus' Looking-glass

Flowering Season: May to September.
Parts of Country Where Found: From British Columbia, Oregon, and Mexico, east to the Atlantic.
Where to Look For: Sterile waste places, dry woods.
For description, habits of growth and seeding, relations with insects, etc., see page 219 of Nature Library volume on WILD FLOWERS.

Betony, Wood (See April)

Black-eyed Susan; Yellow or Ox-eye Daisy

Flowering Season: May to September.
Parts of Country Where Found: Ontario and Northwest Territory to Colorado and Gulf States.
Where to Look For: Open, sunny places; dry fields.
For description, manner of growth, relations with insects, etc., see page 240 of Nature Library volume on WILD FLOWERS. For appearance, identifying colors, etc., see full-color illustration facing page 228.

Blue-eyed Grass, Pointed

Flowering Season: May to August.
Parts of Country Where Found: Newfoundland to British Columbia; the Atlantic to the eastern slope of the Rockies; Virginia to Kansas.
Where to Look For: Moist fields and meadows.
For appearance, color, manner of growth and seeding, etc., see page 31 of Nature Library volume on WILD FLOWERS.

Blackberry, High Bush

Flowering Season: In May and June.
Parts of Country Where Found: New England to Florida, and far westward.
Where to Look For: Dry soil, thickets, fence-rows, waysides, old fields. Low altitudes.
For description, habits of growth and seeding, etc., see page 99 of Nature Library volume on WILD FLOWERS.

Brooklimb, American (See April)

Bunchberry; Low or Dwarf Cornel

Flowering Season: From May to July.
Parts of Country Where Found: Labrador and Alaska to New Jersey and Minnesota.

MAY

Where to Look For: Shadowy, mossy places in cool, rich woods. For appearance, color, description of growing and seeding habits, etc., see page 144 of Nature Library volume on WILD FLOWERS.

Buttercup, Bulbous

Flowering Season: From early May through June.
Parts of Country Where Found: Naturalized from Europe; widespread in U. S. and Canada.
Where to Look For: Fields and roadsides.
For color, appearance, growing habits, etc., see page 58 of Nature Library volume on WILD FLOWERS.

Buttercup, Common Meadow; Tall Crowfoot

Flowering Season: From May to September.
Parts of Country Where Found: Naturalized from Europe in Canada and U. S.; most common in the north.
Where to Look For: Meadows, fields, roadsides, grassy places.
For description, growing habits, etc., see page 57 of Nature Library volume on WILD FLOWERS. For appearance in natural surroundings, see full-color illustration facing page 49.

Buttercup, Swamp or Bush (See April)
Buttercup, Tufted (See April)
Carrion Flower (See April)
Celandine, Greater (See April)
Clover, Common Red (See April)
Columbine, Wild (See April)
Chickweed, Common

Flowering Season: All year.
Parts of Country Where Found: Almost universal.
Where to Look For: Moist, shady soil; woods, meadows.
The sole use man has discovered for this often pestiferous weed with which Nature carpets moist soil the world around is to feed caged song-birds. See page 48 of Nature Library volume on WILD FLOWERS for description.

Clintonia, Yellow

Flowering Season: From May to June.
Parts of Country Where Found: From the Carolinas and Wisconsin far northward (to Labrador).

Where to Look For: Moist, rich, cool woods and thickets.
For appearance, color, growth, and seed habits, etc., see **page 18** of Nature Library volume on WILD FLOWERS.

Clover, White or Dutch

Flowering Season: From May to December.
Parts of Country Where Found: Europe, Asia, and throughout our area.
Where to Look For: Fields, open waste land, cultivated places.
For description, manner of growth, relations to insects, uses, etc., see page 110 of Nature Library volume on WILD FLOWERS.

Daisy, Common, White, or Ox-eye

Flowering Season: May to November.
Parts of Country Where Found: Throughout the U. S. and Canada; not so common in South and West.
Where to Look For: Meadows, pastures, roadsides, waste land.
What is the secret of the daisy's triumphal conquest of our territory? It is because daisies run their business on the principle of a coöperative department store. A long and a merry life to them! A full-color illustration appears facing page 237 of Nature Library volume on WILD FLOWERS, and the structure and habits of this remarkable little flower are described on page 246.

Dogwood, Swamp; or Silky Cornel

Flowering Season: From May to July.
Parts of Country Where Found: New Brunswick and Florida to Nebraska.
Where to Look For: Low wet ground, and beside streams.
For appearance, description of growing and seeding habits, use, etc., see page 145 of Nature Library volume on WILD FLOWERS.

Dogwood, Flowering (See April)

Dutchman's Breeches (See April)

Fleabane, Daisy; Sweet Scabious

Flowering Season: From May to November.
Parts of Country Where Found: Nova Scotia and Virginia to Missouri.
Where to Look For: Fields, waste land, roadsides.
For color, appearance, habits of growth, etc., see page 236 of Nature Library volume on WILD FLOWERS.

MAY

Five-Finger (See April)

Forget-me-not

Flowering Season: From May to July.
Parts of Country Where Found: Native of Europe and Asia; now rapidly spreading from Nova Scotia to New Jersey, Pennsylvania, and beyond.
Where to Look For: Escaped from gardens to brooksides, marshes, and low meadows.
For description of growing habits, relation to insects, etc., see page 182 of Nature Library volume on WILD FLOWERS. For color and appearance in natural surroundings, see full-color illustration facing page 160.

Frost-weed, Long-branched; Frost-flower or Frost-wort; Canadian Rockrose

Flowering Season: Petal-bearing flowers from May to July.
Parts of Country Where Found: New England and the Carolinas to Wisconsin and Kentucky.
Where to Look For: Dry fields, sandy or rocky soil.
For appearance, color, description of growth and seeding habits, etc., see page 131 of Nature Library volume on WILD FLOWERS.

Geranium, Wild (See April)

Gold-thread; Canker-root

Flowering Season: From May to August.
Parts of Country Where Found: Maryland and Minnesota north to circumpolar regions.
Where to Look For: Cool mossy bogs, damp woods.
For description, manner of growth and seeding, uses, etc., see page 68 of Nature Library **volume** on WILD FLOWERS.

Hawthorn, Common; Red Haw; Mayflower

Flowering Season: May.
Parts of Country Where Found: Newfoundland and Manitoba south to the Gulf.
Where to Look For: Thickets, fence-rows, woodland borders.
For appearance, color, habits of growth, etc., see page 97 of Nature Library volume on WILD FLOWERS.

Hellebore, American White; Indian Poke

Flowering Season: From May to July.
Parts of Country Where Found: From ocean to ocean, and from British possessions to Georgia, Tennessee, and Minnesota.
Where to Look For: Swamps, wet woods, low meadows.
For description, growing habits, insect relations, etc., see page 12 of Nature Library volume on WILD FLOWERS.

Hepatica; Liver-Leaf; Liverwort (See March)

Herb Robert

Flowering Season: From May to October.
Parts of Country Where Found: Nova Scotia to Pennsylvania, and west to Missouri.
Where to Look For: Rocky, moist woods and shady roadsides.
For appearance, color, manner of growth and seeding, etc., see page 121 of Nature Library volume on WILD FLOWERS.

Honeysuckle, Wild (See April)

Jack in the Pulpit (See April)

Iris, Blue; Blue Flag, Larger; Fleur-de-Lis

Flowering Season: From May to July.
Parts of Country Where Found: Newfoundland and Manitoba to Arkansas and Florida.
Where to Look For: Marshes, wet meadows.
For description of habits of growth and seeding, relations to insects, etc., see page 27 of Nature Library volume on WILD FLOWERS For appearance in natural surroundings, see full-color illustration on page 16.

Lady's Slipper, Large Yellow; Yellow Moccasin Flower

Flowering Season: From May to July.
Parts of Country Where Found: Nova Scotia and Alabama to Minnesota and Nebraska.
Where to Look For: Moist or boggy woods and thickets; hilly ground.
For description, growth, and seeding habits, relations to insects, etc., see page 32 of Nature Library volume on WILD FLOWERS. For color and appearance see full-color illustration facing page 17.

MAY

Lady's Slipper, Small Yellow

Flowering Season: From May to July.
Parts of Country Where Found: Chiefly along the northern border of U. S. and southern Canada.
Where to Look For: Moist or boggy woods and thickets; hilly ground.
For description, manner of growth and seeding, etc., see page 33 of Nature Library volume on WILD FLOWERS.

Laurel, Mountain or American; Spoon-wood; Broad-leaved Kalmia

Flowering Season: May and June.
Parts of Country Where Found: New Brunswick and Ontario to the Gulf; west to Ohio.
Where to Look For: Sandy or rocky woods, especially in hilly or mountainous country.
For manner of growing, relations to insects, etc., see page 153 of Nature Library volume on WILD FLOWERS. For color and appearance in natural surroundings see full-color illustration facing page 112.

Lupine, Wild; Wild Pea

Flowering Season: May and June.
Parts of Country Where Found: U. S. east of the Mississippi, and eastern Canada.
Where to Look For: Dry, sandy places, banks and hillsides.
For description, manner of growth, interesting habits, etc., see page 105 of Nature Library volume on WILD FLOWERS.

May Apple; Hog Apple; Mandrake

Flowering Season: May.
Parts of Country Where Found: Quebec and the Gulf to Texas and Minnesota.
Where to Look For: Rich, moist woods.
For description, growth habits, fruit, etc., see page 74 of Nature Library volume on WILD FLOWERS. For color and appearance see full-color illustration facing page 69.

Marigold, Marsh (See April)
Meadow Rue, Early (See April)
Mustard, Field or Corn; Charlock or Field Kale

Flowering Season: From May to November.
Parts of Country Where Found: Naturalized from Europe; common.

Where to Look For: Grain fields, gardens, rich waste lands, rubbish heaps.
For appearance, manner of growth, etc., see page 84 of Nature Library volume on WILD FLOWERS.

Mustard, Hedge

Flowering Season: From May to November.
Parts of Country Where Found: Throughout our area.
Where to Look For: Waste places.
For description, growth habits, etc., see page 84 of Nature Library volume on WILD FLOWERS.

Milkwort, Fringed; Polygala

Flowering Season: From May to July.
Parts of Country Where Found: North Canada, south and west to Georgia and Illinois.
Where to Look For: Moist, rich woods, pine lands, light soil.
For description, habits of growing, relations with insects, etc., see Nature Library volume on WILD FLOWERS, page 122.

Moccasin Flower; Pink, Venus', or Stemless Lady's Slipper

Flowering Season: From May to June.
Parts of Country Where Found: Canada and Minnesota to North Carolina and Kentucky.
Where to Look For: Deep, rocky, or sandy woods.
For color, appearance, growth and seeding habits, etc., see page 33 of Nature Library volume on WILD FLOWERS.

New Jersey Tea

Flowering Season: From May to July.
Parts of Country Where Found: Ontario and westward, south to the Gulf of Mexico.
Where to Look For: Dry, open woods and thickets and hillsides.
For description, manner of growth and seeding, uses, etc., see page 126 of Nature Library volume on WILD FLOWERS.

Nightshade; Bittersweet; Blue Bindweed

Flowering Season: From May to September.
Parts of Country Where Found: U. S. east of Kansas, north of New Jersey; Canada, Europe, and Asia.
Where to Look For: Moist thickets, fence rows.

MAY

For description of appearance, manner of growth and seeding, its relation to birds, etc., see page 193 of Nature Library volume on WILD FLOWERS. For color and identifying marks see full-color illustration facing page 192.

Orchis, Showy (See April)

Painted Cup, Scarlet; Indian Paint-brush

Flowering Season: From May to July.
Parts of Country Where Found: Maine and Manitoba to Virginia, Kansas, Texas.
Where to Look For: Meadows, prairies, mountains, moist sandy soil.
For description of appearance, color, manner of growth and seeding, etc., see page 210 of Nature Library volume on WILD FLOWERS.

Partridge Vine (See April)

Pimpernel, Scarlet; Red Chickweed; Poor Man's or Shepherd's Weatherglass or Clock

Flowering Season: May to August.
Parts of Country Where Found: Newfoundland and Florida to Minnesota and Mexico.
Where to Look For: Waste places, dry fields and roadsides, sandy soil.
For appearance, color, description of growth and seeding habits, peculiarities, etc., see page 163 of Nature Library volume on WILD FLOWERS.

Pink, Wild (See April)

Pink, Ground or Moss (See April)

Pitcher-plant

Flowering Season: May and June.
Parts of Country Where Found: Labrador to the Rockies, south to Florida, Kentucky, and Minnesota.
Where to Look For: Peat bogs, spongy, mossy swamps.
For appearance, peculiarities, growth, and relations to insects, etc., see page 84 of Nature Library volume on WILD FLOWERS.

Plantain, Robin's (See April)

Pond Lily (See April)

Rattlesnake-weed; Early or Vein-leaf Hawkweed

Flowering Season: May to October (usually June to September).
Parts of Country Where Found: Maine to Minnesota, south to Georgia.
Where to Look For: Pine woodlands, dry thickets, sandy soil.
For description, manner of growth, etc., see page 259 of Nature Library volume on WILD FLOWERS.

Rose, Swamp

Flowering Season: Late May to midsummer.
Parts of Country Where Found: Quebec to Florida and westward.
Where to Look For: Swamps and low, wet ground.
For appearance, color, manner of growth, etc., see page 102 of Nature Library volume on WILD FLOWERS.

Sarsaparilla, Wild or False

Flowering Season: May and June.
Parts of Country Where Found: Newfoundland to Minnesota and southward.
Where to Look For: Woods, hillsides, thickets.
For description, growth, and seeding habits, uses, etc., see page 140 of Nature Library volume on WILD FLOWERS.

Saxifrage, Early (See March)

Self-heal; Heal-all

Flowering Season: From May to October.
Parts of Country Where Found: North America, Europe, Asia.
Where to Look For: Fields, roadsides, waste places.
For appearance, color, description of growth, etc., see page 188 of Nature Library volume on WILD FLOWERS.

Solomon's Seal (See April)

Shooting Star (See April)

Speedwell, Common

Flowering Season: From May to August.
Parts of Country Where Found: Ontario to Nova Scotia; Michigan and Tennessee eastward. Probably an immigrant from Europe and Asia.
Where to Look For: Dry fields, uplands, open woods.
For appearance, color, manner of growth and seeding, how it got

MAY

its name, relations with insects, etc., see page 204 of Nature Library volume on WILD FLOWERS.

Skullcap, Larger or Hyssop

Flowering Season: From May to August.
Parts of Country Where Found: Southern New England to the Gulf and Texas.
Where to Look For: Tall grass of roadsides and meadows; undergrowth of woods and thickets.
For description, manner of growth, etc., see page 188 of Nature Library volume on WILD FLOWERS.

Spikenard, Wild; False Solomon's Seal

Flowering Season: From May to July.
Parts of Country Where Found: From Nova Scotia and Georgia to British Columbia and Arizona.
Where to Look For: Moist woods, thickets, hillsides.
For appearance, color, growth, and seeding habits, etc., see page 19 of Nature Library volume on WILD FLOWERS.

Spring Beauty; Claytonia (See March)

Star-grass, Yellow

Flowering Season: From May to October.
Parts of Country Where Found: From Maine and the Gulf far westward (to Manitoba).
Where to Look For: Dry, open woods, prairies, grassy waste places, fields.
For description, relations with insects, etc., see page 26 of Nature Library volume on WILD FLOWERS.

Star-flower; Star Anemone

Flowering Season: From May to June.
Parts of Country Where Found: From Virginia and Illinois far north.
Where to Look For: Moist shade of woods and thickets.
For appearance, color, habits of growth, etc., see Nature Library volume on WILD FLOWERS page 162.

Toadflax, Blue or Wild; Linaria

Flowering Season: From May to October.
Parts of Country Where Found: North, Central, and South Americas.

Where to Look For: Dry soil, gravel or sand.
For description of appearance, color, etc., see page 199 of Nature Library volume on WILD FLOWERS.

Trillium, Painted; Painted Wake-Robin

Flowering Season: May to June.
Parts of Country Where Found: Northeastern U. S. Canada westward to Ontario and Missouri, south to Georgia.
Where to Look For: Banks of woodland brooks; cool, moist glens.
For description, see page 22 of Nature Library volume on WILD FLOWERS.

Trillium, Ill-Scented (See April)

Trillium, Nodding; Nodding Wake-Robin (See April)

Violet, Bird's-foot

Flowering Season: Spring, sometimes again in autumn.
Parts of Country Where Found: Maine to Minnesota and southward.
Where to Look For: Shale and sandy soil; hillsides.
For description, growth, habits, insect visitors, etc., see page 132 of Nature Library volume on WILD FLOWERS.

Violet, Lance and Primrose-leaved (See April)

Violet, Downy and Smooth Yellow (See April)

Wake-Robin, Sessile-Flowered (See April)

Wake-Robin, Early or Dwarf; (Trillium) (See March)

Wake-Robin, Large-flowered

Flowering Season: May and June.
Parts of Country Where Found: Vermont and Minnesota to North Carolina and Missouri.
Where to Look For: Damp, rich woods.
For description of growth, habits, etc., see page 22 of Nature Library volume on WILD FLOWERS.

Wood-sorrel, Violet

Flowering Season: May and June.
Parts of Country Where Found: Northern U. S. to the Rockies, south to Florida and New Mexico; more abundant in south.

MAY

Where to Look For: Rocky and sandy woods.
For description of growing habits and interesting peculiarities see page 117 of Nature Library volume on WILD FLOWERS.

Wood-sorrel, White or True

Flowering Season: From May to July.
Parts of Country Where Found: Nova Scotia and Manitoba, south to North Carolina; also a native of Europe.
Where to Look For: Cold, damp woods.
For interesting habits of growth, seeding, and relations to insects see page 115 of Nature Library volume on WILD FLOWERS.

BUTTERFLIES TO BE WATCHED FOR IN MAY

Comma, the Green

The Green Comma is distinctively a northern species—found abundantly in the great regions traversed by the trappers of the Hudson Bay Company. Rare as far south as northern Massachusetts.

They come from their winter quarters in May and commonly continue alive until late in June.

For description, life changes (caterpillar, chrysalis, and mature form), habits of wintering, number of broods produced each season, parts of country where found, favorite food plants, etc., see page 159 of Nature Library volume on BUTTERFLIES.

Dusky-wing, Juvenal's

The species is found from southern New Hampshire west to the Great Plains and south to the Gulf of Mexico. The butterflies appear in open woods and on cut-over lands in May and June.

For description of butterfly, life-history of caterpillar, its food, etc., and other interesting facts, see page 272 of Nature Library volume on BUTTERFLIES.

Fritillary, Meadow

The Meadow Fritillary is common in Canada and the Northern States east of the Rockies. It emerges from the chrysalid late in May.

Article on page 128 of Nature Library volume on BUTTERFLIES describes the interesting developments in the life-history of this butterfly.

Fritillary, Silver-bordered

Widely distributed in North America, being found as far west as the upper Mississippi Valley and the Rocky Mountains, and southward as far as the Carolinas. In New England and the Atlantic States it is one of the commonest of the smaller butterflies.

The first butterflies will be found from late in May to the latter part of June. Second brood of butterflies late in July or early in August. Third brood matures as butterflies in September.

Description of the yearly cycle of this insect will be found on page 131 of Nature Library volume on BUTTERFLIES. For appearance in natural surroundings, characteristic markings, etc., see full-color illustration facing page 145.

Hair-streak, Olive

Along the Atlantic Coast this little butterfly occurs from New Hampshire to Florida and westward to a line drawn from Dakota to Texas.

The species winters in the chrysalis state, the first brood of butterflies bursting forth early in May. In the Northern States, the collector should look for fresh specimens in May and early June and again in July and early August.

For description, characteristic marks of identification, kinds of flowers visited by butterflies and plants upon which eggs are laid, see article on page 249 of Nature Library volume on BUTTERFLIES.

Orange-tip, the Falcate

Generally distributed east of the Rocky Mountains.

In the Northern States the chrysalids remain unchanged until the following spring when the butterflies emerge and are found upon the wing for a few weeks in May and early June. For interesting description and life-history see page 94 of Nature Library volume on BUTTERFLIES.

Painted Lady or the Cosmopolite also called Thistle Butterfly

The universal distribution of the thistle upon which this butterfly depends for food has led to a like distribution of the insect itself. They begin to be seen in fields and along roadsides about the middle of May.

On page 167 of the Nature Library volume on BUTTERFLIES there is given a description of the Painted Lady, its life-changes, its remarkable powers of flight, etc., and in a full-color illustra-

MAY

tion facing page 177 its coloring and characteristic markings are shown.

Red Admiral or Nettle Butterfly

The middle of May one may see in open fields and along sunny highways these Red Admirals flitting from flower to flower.

Late in May and early in June they deposit their eggs upon the leaves of the nettles. The eggs that were laid in May develop into butterflies during July.

This butterfly is found in practically all localities where nettles grow.

A description of its life changes, the leaf nests made by its caterpillar, its enemies among insects, etc., will be found on page 160 of Nature Library volume on BUTTERFLIES. Facing page 176 is a full-color illustration of the Red Admiral in its natural surroundings.

Skipper, Roadside

This little butterfly is found apparently in most parts of the United States, as it has been collected in New England, California, Texas, and many intermediate points. It appears in May and early June.

Its appearance, characteristic markings, life history, etc., are described on page 280 of Nature Library volume on BUTTERFLIES.

Skipper, Tawny-edged

Found from Nova Scotia to British Columbia, south along the Rocky Mountains to New Mexico, Texas, and Florida.

Butterflies come from the liberated chrysalids in May or June. They remain upon the wing for several weeks so that worn specimens may be taken late in July or, rarely, even early in August.

A description of this butterfly and its life history may be found in article beginning on page 279 of Nature Library volume on BUTTERFLIES.

Swallowtail, Black

Found throughout many months of the year in practically all parts of North America south of Canada.

The larva which goes into the chrysalis in September does not come out as a butterfly until the following May or June.

The coloring, identifying marks of both larvæ and adult insects, together with the other important facts in the life history of the Black Swallowtail will be found in the description given on page 59 of Nature Library volume on BUTTERFLIES.

Swallowtail, Green-clouded

Essentially a southern species found over a wide range of territory from the Misssissippi River to the Atlantic Ocean. Occurs as far north as New Hampshire and Vermont.

Passes through the winter in the chrysalis stage. Late in spring the butterflies emerge and soon afterward lay their eggs singly upon the leaves of sassafras or spice bush. The butterflies of the second brood of the season are likely to appear in August, continuing to become more abundant throughout that month. They become full grown during September or October, and then change to chrysalids which remain dormant until the following spring.

Open groves, the borders of woods, and the margins of streams or marshes are the places where one is most likely to find spice bush and sassafras.

For the interesting description and history of this butterfly see page 67 of the Nature Library volume on BUTTERFLIES.

Swallowtail, Palamedes

Distinctly a southern form occurring as far west as the Mississippi River throughout the more southern states. Several broods each year.

On page 76 of the Nature Library volume on BUTTERFLIES there is given the story of the life changes of the Palamedes Swallowtail, with a description of its appearance and identifying marks.

Swallowtail, Tiger

Occurs over a very large part of the North American continent, being found from ocean to ocean and from Canada to Florida.

Passes the winter as a chrysalis, the butterflies coming forth just about the time that the lilacs bloom. They remain upon the wing for a few weeks and deposit their eggs upon a great variety of trees and shrubs.

Then fully developed they change to chrysalids which give forth the summer brood of butterflies in July and August.

For a full description of this beautiful butterfly, and of its fascinating larvæ with the "mask-like face" and other peculiarities, see the article beginning on page 72 of the Nature Library volume on BUTTERFLIES. A full-color illustration of the Tiger Swallowtail is to be found on page 65.

Violet-tip

The adult butterflies appear in fields and pastures in May.
A description of the Violet-tip with its interesting life changes,

MAY

its preferred foods, etc., together with the quaint fancies with which tradition has associated it, is found in article beginning on page 150 of the Nature Library volume on BUTTERFLIES. A full-color illustration will be found on page 161.

White Butterfly, Grey-veined

In the case of the Grey-veined White, we collect in early spring in New England, or other northern states, a lot of chrysalids.
Description, identifying marks and story of its life changes will be found on page 87 of the Nature Library volume on BUTTERFLIES.

Wood Satyr, the Little

Often found in fields and along hedge rows rather than in the woods.
General distribution west to the Mississippi Valley, extending from the corner of Dakota, south through Nebraska, Kansas and central Texas, and north to Wisconsin, Michigan, and New England. It occupies the whole of the United States east and south of the lines thus indicated.
Butterflies appear in May and early June.
Described in Nature Library volume on BUTTERFLIES, on page 226.

TREES TO BE NOTICED IN MAY

Eastern Mountain Ash

The flat-topped cluster of creamy white flowers appears in May and June, above the dark yellow-green foliage; and the scarlet berries, ripe in September, when the leaves have turned yellow, may persist till spring.
For description, habits of growth, flowering, seeding, etc., see page 116 of Nature Library volume on TREES. Facing page 124 will be found a full-color illustration, showing the beautiful appearance of this tree in its natural surroundings.

The White Ash

Ash trees are late in coming into leaf. Not until May do the rusty yellow winter buds of the white ash swell and throw out on separate trees their staminate and pistillate flower clusters.
For description of appearance and growing habits of tree, season of flowering, leaving and seeding, details of leaf, etc., see page 202

of Nature Library volume on TREES. A full-color illustration appears facing page 201.

The Horse-chestnut

The glory of the horse-chestnut comes at blooming time, when the upturning branches, like the arms of a candelabrum, are each tipped with a white blossom cluster, pointed like a candle flame. For appearance of tree and blossoms, habits of growth, kind of country where found, etc., see page 65 of Nature Library volume on TREES. Facing page 40 is a full-color illustration showing the horse-chestnut tree in bloom.

The Fringe Tree

In May and June the tree is decked with a bridal veil of white that makes it one of the most ethereal and the most elegant of lawn and park trees at this supreme moment of the year.
On page 126 of the Nature Library volume on TREES there is given a description of this tree, its habits of growth, leaving and flowering, seeding, etc., and parts of the country where it is found.

The Hemlock

In May the new blossoms sprinkle all the leafy twigs—the staminate, yellow; the pistillate, pale violet.
For description of growing habits, seasons of flowering and leaving, seed and fruit, etc., see page 260 of Nature Library volume on TREES.

The Black Locust

In late May the tree-top bursts into bloom that is often so profuse as to whiten the whole mass of the dainty foliage.
A description of this tree, its leafage and foliage, its insect visitors and arch insect enemy will be found on page 178 of the Nature Library volume on TREES.

The Mesquite

Greenish fragrant flowers, thickly set in finger-like clusters, appear in successive crops from May to July.
On page 188 of the Nature Library volume on TREES appears a description of the mesquite, and an account of its numerous uses to man and beast. A full-color illustration, with details also of leaf, catkins, and pod, will be found facing page 185.

MAY

The Mockernut

The flowers are abundant, and yet the most surprising show of colors on this tree comes not in May, when it blossoms, but in April when the great buds swell. The outer scales fall, and the inner ones expand into ruddy silken sheathes that stand erect around the central cluster of leaves, not yet awake, and every branch seems to hold up a great red tulip! The sight is wonderful. Nothing looks more flowerlike than these opening hickory buds, and to the unobserving passerby the transformation is nothing short of a miracle. In a day, the leaves rise and spread their delicate leaflets, lengthening and becoming smooth, as the now useless red scales fall in a shower to the ground.

A full description of the mockernut appears on page 40 of the Nature Library volume on TREES.

The Red Oak

The bloom is very abundant and conspicuous, the fringe-like pollen-bearing aments four and five inches long, drooping from the twigs in clusters, when the leaves are half grown in May.

A full description of this tree, its leafage and bloom and other marks of identification, is to be found on page 62 of the Nature Library volume on TREES.

The White Oak

The supreme moment in the white oak's year comes in spring, when the gray old tree awakes, the buds swell and cast off their brown scales, and the young leaves appear.

The details of this lovely sight, together with other facts regarding the white oak, are to be found on page 49 of the Nature Library volume on TREES. A full-color illustration, together with detail of leaf and acorn, will be found facing page 25.

The White Pine

If it is spring, note that the terminal bud of this tree has pushed out, and around it five-clustered buds are forming a circle of shoots. In autumn, after the season's growth is finished, each twig ends in a single bud, with a whorl of five buds around it. From the ground upward, count the platforms of branches. Each whorl of five marks a year in the tree's growth. Read the age of the tree by the platforms of branches on the trunk.

For a description of the white pine, its leafage and catkins and cones, and other interesting facts regarding it, see page 222 of the

Nature Library volume on TREES. A full-color illustration, together with detail of leaf and cone, will be found facing page 217.

The Silver Bell Tree

This tree earns its name in May, when among the green leaves the clustered bell flowers gradually pale from green to white, with rosy tints that seem to come from the ruddy flower-stems.

Its growth habits, its geographic distribution and decorative uses are noted in the Nature Library on TREES on page 123.

ANIMALS TO BE NOTED IN MAY

Virginia Deer

Up to the month of January, the does and bucks are still in company in the deer-yards.

May sees the doe a renovated animal and also sees her alone. About the middle of the month she gives birth to her young.

For description, habits of mating, favorite food supply, parts of country where found, usual home surroundings, etc., see page 9 of the Nature Library volume on ANIMALS. For color and appearance in natural surroundings see full-color illustration facing page 3.

Common Mole

In winter the mole avoids the frost by digging much deeper. In the spring and perhaps again in the autumn the litter of young moles is produced in the warmly lined central chamber.

For description of seasonal activities, habits of mating and wintering, food, etc., see page 258 of Nature Library volume on ANIMALS. For appearance in natural surrounding, see full-color illustration facing page 255.

Raccoon

The time of mating is not certainly known but is probably in the autumn. The young are born in April or May, four being the usual number.

By late June they are a third grown, and begin to sit outside the den on bright days.

Frogs are thought by many observers to be the summer-long main support of raccoons.

A description of the habits, shelter, seasonal activities, etc., of the raccoon, will be found on page 227 of the Nature Library volume on ANIMALS. A full-color illustration facing page 227 shows its color and appearance in natural surroundings.

June, The Rose Moon

By June all the birds which migrate southward for the winter months have appeared in their summer haunts farther north, and are busily engaged in the domestic adventure of raising a family. If you are fortunate enough to live in the country, or in the outskirts of a small town, you can fill this whole month's spare time with the keen pleasures of discovery, simply by making a June list of the kinds of birds which have nests in your neighborhood—say within a quarter mile of your home.

When you set out seriously to identify and list the varieties, with the aid of your bird volume and an opera glass, you will be indeed surprised at the number. Even if you live in a big city, with your field of nature study limited to a city park, you will have the chance to see and name a goodly variety of wild species in this month when parenthood is the chief occupation of birddom.

Mr. Dallas Lore Sharp, popular nature writer, kept track of the birds nesting in June within singing distance of his Massachusetts farmhouse, and found thirty-six species.

"This is not a modern natural history story," he writes in his book, 'The Lay of the Land,' "an extraordinary discovery that only I am capable of making. Start your own June list, and I warrant you will find as many. Any place that offers a fair chance to the native birds will keep you busy counting nests in June."

In the chimney of Mr. Sharp's house three or

four families of swifts built their nests; in the loft of his barn were a small colony of barn swallows; and under the roof of the pig-pen nested a pair of phœbes.

Along the steep southern slope between his house and orchard nested a pair of indigo buntings and a pair of rose-breasted grosbeaks; also, in the thick underbrush he found chewinks, thrashers, black-and-white warblers, song sparrows, and a pair of partridges.

In his orchard there were half a dozen chippies' nests, even more robins', two nests of bluebirds, and one each of the tree swallow, flicker, yellow warbler, chebec, downy woodpecker, kingbird, great-crested flycatcher, redstart, and screech owl.

The Yellow Warbler

Baltimore orioles nested in the elms along the road; close to the little river were the nests of catbirds and redwinged blackbirds; a nest of swamp sparrows and of Maryland yellow throats were in the meadow, and in the woodlot a pewee's nest, a crow's nest, and three nests of oven birds.

Mr. Sharp found the nests of all these birds, and in addition knew that several species had their homes near, among them the yellow-billed cuckoo, the blue jay, wood-thrush, and chestnut-sided warbler.

If you identify only half or a third of these species in the vicinity of your home, and succeed in seeing only a few nests, you will find an immense satisfaction in doing it.

But your hobby may be wild flowers, or butterflies, and in either case, June offers you so many that you will want to spend every leisure hour in becoming familiar with their fascinating beauties.

In June it is not a case of searching out a few shy arbutus blossoms, or hepaticas, in the shade of damp woods, but a question of choosing, from wide-flung meadows spread with bloom, the flowers that interest you most.

When you walk abroad in June, you do not go to some half-hidden haunt of rare flowers, but through pastures drifted white with daisies, meadows golden with buttercups, and over rolling woodland hillsides gorgeous with the massed pink of laurel.

"What is so rare as a day in June?" and what is so pleasant as the ability to call a few of such a day's striking floral beauties by name, and understand to some extent the wonderfully fascinating ways in which they live and continue from season to season?

Take as an example the evening primrose. Seen by the dusty roadside, on some hot June afternoon, it presents a jaded, bedraggled appearance. At the top are its erect, unopened buds, below them are one or two recently faded flowers, and still lower down a few badly wilted ones. Is the whole plant perishing from lack of water? Why are there no open flowers visible?

Let us mark the plant with a bit of string and come back to this same flower after sunset, in the twilight. We shall see a striking change. At sunset, one of the buds at the top began to expand its delicate petals and is now open.

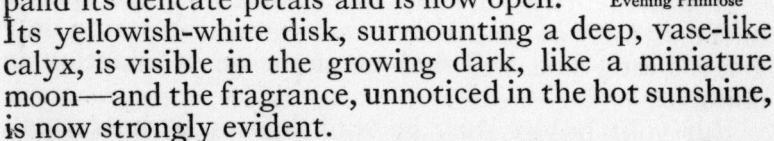

Evening Primrose

Its yellowish-white disk, surmounting a deep, vase-like calyx, is visible in the growing dark, like a miniature moon—and the fragrance, unnoticed in the hot sunshine, is now strongly evident.

Why does it come out with its full beauty only **at**

night? Let us wait here on a convenient stone and see if the mystery will solve itself. Soon there is a fluttering in the dusk, and an exquisite little rose-pink sphinx moth, his wings bordered with yellow, settles upon our just-opened primrose flower. If it was not so dark, we might see him uncoil his long tongue, or sucking tube, and send it deep down into the flower's heart for the nectar stored there. He stays only a moment, but during that time some of the sticky yellow pollen dust, placed upon his body by some other primrose, has been brushed off and now adheres to the pistil of this individual flower we are watching. The nectar, the perfume, the white, easily seen petals, all are to attract the moth, in order that the flower may be fertilized with pollen from another distant plant and thereby produce seed. The moth's work once done, this particular flower will fade. To-morrow morning it will be closed and wilted; and to-morrow night another of the buds will open its delights to lure another sphinx moth.

The Sphinx Moth

But what happens if a moth fails to come during the night? Something really remarkable! When you hear what it is, you will be almost willing to believe that the evening primrose plant really *thinks*, and acts accordingly. Your Nature Library volume on Wild Flowers will give you the answer to this and many other fascinating questions.

June is the high-tide of the year's life. Whether you are interested in birds, flowers, butterflies, trees or animals, you will be kept busy this month, and if you go upon your walks armed with even a little knowledge of what to look for, you will enjoy your stroll much more, and besides, you will soon have a store of summer memories far richer than you ever had before.

JUNE

WILD FLOWERS APPEARING IN JUNE

Arethusa; Indian Pink (See May)

Anemone, Wood (See April)

Barberry; Pepperidge Bush (See May)

Baneberry, White (See April)

Beard-tongue, Hairy (See May)

Bellflower, Clasping; Venus' Looking Glass (See May)

Betony, Wood (See April)

Bluets (See April)

Bergamot, Wild

Flowering Season: From June to September.
Parts of Country Where Found: Eastern Canada and Minnesota to the Gulf of Mexico.
Where to Look For: Open woods, thickets, dry rocky hills.
For description, habits of growth, and seeding, etc., see page 192 of Nature Library volume on WILD FLOWERS.

Bindweed, Hedge or Great; Wild Morning-glory

Flowering Season: From June to September.
Parts of Country Where Found: Nova Scotia and North Carolina to Nebraska; Europe and Asia.
Where to Look For: Wayside hedges, thickets, fields, walls.
Description of this flower, growth and seeding habits, insect visitors, etc., see page 177 of Nature Library volume on WILD FLOWERS.

Black-eyed Susan; Yellow or Ox-eyed Daisy (See May)

Blue-eyed Grass, Pointed (See May)

Blackberry, High Bush (See May)

Brooklime, American (See April)

Bouncing Bet; Soapwort

Flowering Season: June to September.
Parts of Country Where Found: Generally common; **naturalized** from Europe.
Where to Look For: Roadsides, banks, waste places.

A description of this plant, with its uses, etc., will be found on page 52 of Nature Library volume on WILD FLOWERS.

Bugloss; Viper's; Blue-weed; Blue Thistle or Devil

Flowering Season: June and July.
Parts of Country Where Found: New Brunswick and Virginia to Nebraska; Europe and Asia.
Where to Look For: Dry fields, waste places, roadsides.
A description of this flower, with the folk lore attached to it, is given on page 184 of Nature Library volume on WILD FLOWERS.

Bunchberry; Low or Dwarf Cornel (see May)

Buttercup, Bulbous (see May)

Buttercup, Common Meadow; Tall Crowfoot (see May)

Butterfly-weed; Orange Milkweed

Flowering Season: June to September.
Parts of Country Where Found: Maine and Ontario to the Gulf and Arizona.
Where to Look For: Dry or sandy fields, hills, roadsides.
This flower, its distinguishing features, its many insect visitors and its uses are described in article on page 176 of the Nature Library volume on WILD FLOWERS.

Button-bush; Honey-balls; Button-ball Shrub

Flowering Season: From June to September.
Parts of Country Where Found: New Brunswick to Florida and Cuba, west to Arizona and California.
Where to Look For: Beside streams and ponds, swamps, low ground.
For description of appearance, color, and identifying marks, see page 215 of Nature Library volume on WILD FLOWERS.

Calapogon; Grass Pink

Flowering Season: June to July.
Parts of Country Where Found: Newfoundland to Florida; west to the Mississippi.
Where to Look For: Swamps, cranberry bogs, low meadows.
A description of this lovely wild orchid, which is, fortunate, far from rare, is to be found on page 41 of the Nature Library volume on WILD FLOWERS.

JUNE

Campion, Starry

Flowering Season: June to August.
Parts of Country Where Found: Rhode Island and the Carolinas to the Mississippi and Arkansas.
Where to Look For: Woods; shady banks.
This flower is fully described and its interesting relation to insects noted in article on page 50 of the Nature Library volume on WILD FLOWERS.

Carrion Flower (See April)

Carrot, Wild; Queen Anne's Lace

Flowering Season: June to September.
Parts of Country Where Found: Eastern half of the U. S. and Canada; Europe and Asia
Where to Look For: Waste lands, fields, roadsides.
This "pest to farmers, joy to the flower-lover, and welcome signal for refreshment to hosts of flies, beetles, bees, and wasps" is described on page 142 of Nature Library volume on WILD FLOWERS.

Celandine, Greater (See April)

Chickweed (See May)

Clintonia, Yellow (see May)[1]

Clover, Yellow Sweet; Yellow Melilot

Flowering Season: Summer and fall.
Parts of Country Where Found: Naturalized from Europe; common.
Where to Look For: Waste places.
Description and peculiarities noted on page 109 of Nature Library volume on WILD FLOWERS.

Clover, White or Dutch (See May)

Clover, White Sweet; White Melilot

Flowering Season: June to November.
Parts of Country Where Found: United States, Europe, Asia.
Where to Look For: Waste lands; roadsides.
For description of this flower see page 109 of Nature Library volume on WILD FLOWERS.

Cohosh, Black; Black Snakeroot

Flowering Season: June to August.
Parts of Country Where Found: Maine and Georgia to Ontario and Missouri.
Where to Look For: Rich woods and woodland borders; hillsides. For description of this flower, its growth and seeding habits, insect visitors, etc., see page 71 of Nature Library volume on WILD FLOWERS.

Columbine, Wild (See April)

Culver's-root or Physic

Flowering Season: June to September.
Parts of Country Where Found: Nova Scotia and Alabama to Nebraska.
Where to Look For: Rich, moist woods, thickets, meadows.
For description, habits of growth, etc., see page 206 of Nature Library volume on WILD FLOWERS.

Day-flower, Virginia or Common

Flowering Season: From June to September.
Parts of Country Where Found: Southern New York to Illinois and Michigan, Nebraska, Texas, and through tropical America to Paraguay.
Where to Look For: Moist, shady ground.
For description of flower see page 10 of Nature Library volume on WILD FLOWERS.

Daisy, Common (See May)

Dogbane, Spreading or Fly-trap

Flowering Season: June and July.
Parts of Country Where Found: Northern part of British possessions south to Georgia; west to Nebraska.
Where to Look For: Fields, thickets, beside roads, lanes and walls. For a description of this flower and its interesting relations with the insect world see article on page 169 of Nature Library volume on WILD FLOWERS.

Dogwood, Swamp; Silky Cornel (See May)

Five Finger (See April)

Fleabane, Daisy; Sweet Scabious (see May)

JUNE

Forget-Me-Not (See May)

Frost-weed, Hoary

Flowering Season: June and July.
Parts of Country Where Found: New England and the Carolinas to Wisconsin and Kentucky.
Where to Look For: Dry fields, sandy or rocky soil.
For description, growth, and seeding habits, etc., see page 131 of Nature Library volume on WILD FLOWERS.

Frost-weed, Long Branched Frost-flower or Frost-wort; Canadian Rock Rose (See May)

Geranium, Wild (See April)

Gold-Thread; Canker Root (See May)

Golden-Rod, Early, Plume, or Sharp-toothed

Flowering Season: June to November.
Parts of Country Where Found: North Carolina and Missouri very far north.
Where to Look For: Dry, rocky soil.
A description of this flower will be found on page 228 of Nature Library volume on WILD FLOWERS.

Harebell or Hairbell

Flowering Season: June to September.
Parts of Country Where Found: Arctic regions of all continents; south on all continents, through Canada to New Jersey and Pennsylvania; west to Nebraska, to Arizona in the Rockies, and to California in the Sierra Nevadas.
Where to Look For: Moist rocks, uplands.
Article describing the Harebell will be found on page 218 of Nature Library volume on WILD FLOWERS.

Hawkweed, Orange or Tawny

Flowering Season: June to September.
Parts of Country Where Found: Pennsylvania and Middle States to British possessions.
Where to Look For: Fields, woods, roadsides, dry places.
The appearance, color, and manner of growth of this flower will be found described on page 258 of the Nature Library volume on WILD FLOWERS.

Hellebore, American White; Indian Poke (See May)

Herb Robert (See May)

Indian Pipe; Ice-plant; Ghost-flower; Corpse-plant

Flowering Season: June to August.
Parts of Country Where Found: Almost throughout temperate North America.
Where to Look For: Heavily shaded, moist, rich woods, especially under oak and pine trees.
An interesting description of this uncanny-looking flower will be found on page 147 of Nature Library volume on WILD FLOWERS and a full-color illustration facing page 101 shows its startling appearance in natural surroundings.

Indigo, Wild; Yellow or Indigo Broom

Flowering Season: June to September
Parts of Country Where Found: Maine and Minnesota to the Gulf States.
Where to Look For: Dry, sandy soil.
Description of this flower, its insect visitors, etc., will be found on page 104 of Nature Library volume on WILD FLOWERS.

Iris, Blue; Larger Blue Flag; Fleur-de-Lis (See May)

Jamestown Weed; Jimson Weed; Thorn Apple

Flowering Season: June to September.
Parts of Country Where Found: Nova Scotia to the Gulf and west beyond the Mississippi.
Where to Look For: Light soil, fields, waste land near dwellings, rubbish heaps.
A full description of this flower, its relations in the flower world, its uses to man, etc., will be found on page 194 of the Nature Library volume on WILD FLOWERS.

Jack in the Pulpit (See April)

Lady's Slipper, Large Yellow; Yellow Moccasin Flower (See May)

Lady's Slipper, Small Yellow (See May)

Laurel, Mountain or American Spoonwood, Broad-Leaved Kalmia (See May)

JUNE

Laurel, Sheep; Narrow-leaved Laurel

Flowering Season: June and July.
Parts of Country Where Found: Labrador to Ontario and southward.
Where to Look For: Moist fields or swampy ground, or hillsides.
A description of this plant will be found on page 156 of Nature Library volume on WILD FLOWERS.

Lily, Blackberry

Flowering Season: June and July.
Parts of Country Where Found: Connecticut to Georgia, west to Indiana and Missouri.
Where to Look For: Roadsides and hills.
This lovely lily, a native of China, is described on page 29 of Nature Library volume on WILD FLOWERS.

Lily, Red, Wood, or Flame

Flowering Season: June and July.
Parts of Country Where Found: Nortnern border of U. S., west to Ontario, south to the Carolinas and West Virginia.
Where to Look For: Dry woods, sandy soil, borders, and thickets.
A description of this beautiful lily will be found on page 16 of Nature Library volume on WILD FLOWERS.

Lily, Water; Sweet Scented White Pond Lily

Flowering Season: June to September.
Parts of Country Where Found: Nova Scotia and the Gulf to the Mississippi.
Where to Look For: Still water, ponds, lakes, slow streams.
"Sumptuous queen of our native aquatic plants" to which "man, beast, and insect pay grateful homage," this lily is described on page 55 of the Nature Library volume on WILD FLOWERS, and a full-color illustration given facing page 48.

Lily, Pond; Large Yellow (See April)

Lily, Wild Yellow, Meadow, Field, or Canada

Flowering Season: June and July.
Parts of Country Where Found: Nova Scotia to Georgia, and westward beyond the Mississippi.
Where to Look For: Swamps, low meadows. moist fields.

Description will be found on page 14 of the Nature Library volume on WILD FLOWERS, and the color and appearance of this lovely flower in its natural surroundings is shown in full-color illustration facing page 4.

Lettuce, Tall or Wild; Horse-weed

Flowering Season: June to November.
Parts of Country Where Found: Georgia and Arkansas to British possessions.
Where to Look For: Moist, open ground; roadsides.
This flower is described and its uses noted in article on page 257 of Nature Library volume on WILD FLOWERS.

Loosestrife, Four-leaved or Whorled

Flowering Season: June to August.
Parts of Country Where Found: Georgia and Illinois north to New Brunswick.
Where to Look For: Open woodland, thickets, roadsides, moist, sandy soil.
This flower is described and the ancient superstition which attaches to it related on page 161 of the Nature Library volume on WILD FLOWERS.

Lupine, Wild; Wild Pea (See May)

Marigold, Marsh (See April)

Meadow-sweet

Flowering Season: June to August.
Parts of Country Where Found: Newfoundland and Georgia to the Rockies; Europe and Asia.
Where to Look For: Low meadows, swamps, ditches, fence-rows.
This flower, which is visited by many insects, is described on page 96 of Nature Library volume on WILD FLOWERS.

Milkweed, Common; Common Silkweed

Flowering Season: June to September.
Parts of Country Where Found: New Brunswick and North Carolina to Kansas.
Where to Look For: Fields and waste places, roadsides.
This flower, with its marvellously perfected mechanism for fertilization, is rich in nectar upon which bees, wasps, flies, butterflies, and beetles come to feast. Full description is given on page 171

JUNE

of Nature Library volume on WILD FLOWERS, and a full-color illustration is to be found facing page 129.

Milkwort, Common, Field, or Purple; Purple Polygala

Flowering Season: June to September.
Parts of Country Where Found: Southern Canada to North Carolina, and west to the Mississippi.
Where to Look For: Fields and meadows, moist or sandy.
Description, with tradition noted from which the name milkwort is derived, will be found on page 123 of Nature Library volume on WILD FLOWERS.

Milkwort, Fringed; Polygala (See May)

Monkey-flower

Flowering Season: June to September.
Parts of Country Where Found: Manitoba, Nebraska, and Texas to the Atlantic.
Where to Look For: Swamps, beside streams and ponds.
Described on page 203 of the Nature Library volume on WILD FLOWERS.

Moccasin Flower; Pink, Venus' or Stemless Lady's Slipper
(See May)

Motherwort

Flowering Season: June to September.
Parts of Country Where Found: Naturalized from Europe and Asia. Nova Scotia and North Carolina to Minnesota and Nebraska.
Where to Look For: Waste places near dwellings.
This flower, which the bees love well, is described on page 189 of Nature Library volume on WILD FLOWERS.

Mullein, Great; Velvet or Flannel Plant; Mullein Dock

Flowering Season: June to September.
Parts of Country Where Found: Minnesota and Kansas to Nova Scotia and Florida; Europe.
Where to Look For: Dry fields, banks, stony waste land.
This plant, from which humming-birds have been detected gathering hairs to line their tiny nests, is described on page 196 of Nature Library volume on WILD FLOWERS.

NATURE'S PROGRAM

Mullein, Moth

Flowering Season: June to November.
Parts of Country Where Found: Naturalized from Europe and Asia; more or less common throughout Canada and the United States.
Where to Look For: Dry, open waste land; roadsides; fields.
Described on page 198 of the Nature Library volume on WILD FLOWERS.

Mustard, Black

Flowering Season: June to November.
Parts of Country Where Found: Naturalized from Europe and Asia; common throughout our area.
Where to Look For: Roadsides, fields, neglected gardens.
This plant, whose tiny dark brown seeds are "sharper than the serpent's tooth" is described on page 82 of Nature Library volume on WILD FLOWERS.

Mustard, Field or Corn; Charlock or Field Kale (See May)

Mustard, Hedge (See May)

New Jersey Tea (See May)

Nightshade; Bittersweet; Blue Bindweed (See May)

Orchis, Showy (See April)

Orchis, Large, or Early, Purple-fringed

Flowering Season: June to August.
Parts of Country Where Found: New Brunswick to Ontario; south to North Carolina; west to Michigan.
Where to Look For: Rich, moist meadows, muddy places, woods.
A fascinating description of the manner in which this flower's marvellous mechanism adapts itself to its insect benefactors is to be found on page 36 of the Nature Library volume on WILD FLOWERS.

Painted Cup, Scarlet; Indian Paint Brush (See May)

Parsnip, Wild or Field

Flowering Season: June to September.
Parts of Country Where Found: Europe; nearly throughout the United States.
Where to Look For: Waste places, roadsides, fields.

JUNE

This flower, which intelligent cattle avoid, is described on page 141 of the Nature Library volume on WILD FLOWERS.

Partridge Vine (See April)

Pickerel Weed

Flowering Season: June to October.
Parts of Country Where Found: Eastern half of U. S. and Canada.
Where to Look For: Shallow water of ponds and streams.
This flower amongst whose leaves backwoodsmen say that pickerel lay their eggs, is described on page 11 of the Nature Library volume on WILD FLOWERS.

Pimpernel, Scarlet; Red Chickweed; Poor Man's or Shepherd's Weather Glass or Clock (See May)

Pine Sap; False Beech-drops

Flowering Season: June to October.
Parts of Country Where Found: Florida and Arizona, far northward into British Possessions; Europe and Asia.
Where to Look For: Dry woods, especially under firs, beeches, and oaks.
This plant, "branded a sinner, through its loss of leaves and honest green coloring matter," is described on page 149 of Nature Library volume on WILD FLOWERS.

Pitcher Plant (See May)

Pink, Swamp; Swamp Honeysuckle; White or Clammy Azalea

Flowering Season: June and July.
Parts of Country Where Found: Maine to Florida and west to Texas, chiefly near the coast.
Where to Look For: Low, wet places.
Description of this flower will be found on page 151 of the Nature Library volume on WILD FLOWERS.

Pink, Wild (See April)

Pink, Ground or Moss (See April)

Pipsissewa; Prince's Pine

Flowering Season: June to August.
Parts of Country Where Found: British Possessions and the U. S. north of Georgia from coast to coast. Also Mexico, Europe, Asia.

Where to Look For: Dry woods, sandy leaf mould.
A description of this flower is given on page 145 of Nature Library volume on WILD FLOWERS.

Plantain, Robin's (See April)

Poke-weed; Scoke; Pigeon-berry; Ink-berry; Garget

Flowering Season: June to October.
Parts of Country Where Found: Maine and Ontario to Florida and Texas.
Where to Look For: Roadsides, thickets, field borders and waste soil, especially in burnt-over districts.
On the fruit, robins, flickers, chewinks, downy woodpeckers and many other birds, may be found feeding, whose undigested seeds these birds will disperse far and wide. A description of this interesting wild plant is given on page 47 of the Nature Library volume on WILD FLOWERS.

Primrose, Evening

Flowering Season: June to October.
Parts of Country Where Found: Labrador to the Gulf, west to the Rockies.
Where to Look For: Roadsides, dry fields, thickets, fence corners.
This flower, with its interesting habits, its relations with insects, etc., is described on page 137 of the Nature Library volume on WILD FLOWERS. A full-color illustration appears facing page 100.

Rattlesnake Weed; Early or Vein Leaf Hawkweed (See May)

Raspberry, Purple-flowering or Virginia

Flowering Season: June to August.
Parts of Country Where Found: Northern Canada; Georgia to Michigan and Tennessee.
Where to Look For: Rocky woods, dells, shady roadsides.
A description of this plant, its flower, leaf, and other means of identification will be found on page 100 of Nature Library volume on WILD FLOWERS.

Rhododendron, American or Great; Great Laurel

Flowering Season: June to July.
Parts of Country Where Found: Uncommon from Ohio and New

JUNE

England to Nova Scotia; abundant through the Alleghenies to Georgia.
Where to Look For: Mountainous woodland, hillsides near streams.
For description of this plant, its habits of growth, effects on insect visitors, etc., see page 152 of Nature Library volume on WILD FLOWERS. For appearance, color, and identifying details, see full-color illustration facing page 109.

Rose, Smoother, Early, or Meadow

Flowering Season: June and July.
Parts of Country Where Found: Newfoundland and New Jersey to beyond the Mississippi.
Where to Look For: Moist, rocky places.
For description of this flower, means of identification, etc., see page 102 of Nature Library volume on WILD FLOWERS.

Rose, Swamp (See May)

Saint John's-Wort, Common

Flowering Season: June to September.
Parts of Country Where Found: Throughout our area, except the extreme north; Europe and Asia.
Where to Look For: Fields, waste lands, roadsides.
A description of this naturalized immigrant, with an account of the tradition that gives the flower its name, is to be found on page 129 of the Nature Library volume on WILD FLOWERS.

Sarsaparilla, Wild or False (See May)

Self-Heal; Heal-All (See May)

Solomon's Seal, Hairy or True (See April)

Speedwell, Common (See May)

Skullcap, Larger or Hyssop (See May)

Spikenard, Wild; False Solomon's Seal (See May)

Squirrel Corn

Flowering Season: May to June.
Parts of Country Where Found: Nova Scotia and Virginia to the Mississippi.
Where to Look For: Rich, moist woods.

For description and means of identification, see page 80 of Nature Library volume on WILD FLOWERS.

Star Grass, Yellow (See May)

Star Flower; Star Anemone (See May)

Sweetbrier or Eglantine

Flowering Season: June and July.
Parts of Country Where Found: Eastern Canada to Virginia and Tennessee.
Where to Look For: Dry, rocky pastures and waste places.
Means of identifying this lovely little flower are given on page 103 of Nature Library volume on WILD FLOWERS.

Toadflax, Blue or Wild; Linaria (See May)

Trillium, Painted; Painted Wake Robin (See May)

Trillium, Nodding; Nodding Wake Robin (See April)

Trillium, Purple (See April)

Vervain, Blue; Wild Hyssop

Flowering Season: June to September.
Parts of Country Where Found: Almost throughout U. S. and Canada.
Where to Look For: Moist meadows, roadsides, waste places.
For a description of this flower, its insect visitors, and the traditions clinging to its name, see page 185 of Nature Library volume on WILD FLOWERS. For color and appearance in natural surroundings, see full-color illustration facing page 176.

Vetch, Blue, Tufted, or Cow; Tare

Flowering Season: June to August.
Parts of Country Where Found: U. S. from New Jersey, Kentucky, and Iowa northward and northwestward.
Where to Look For: Dry soil, fields, waste lands.
This flower is described and the habits of its insect visitors related on page 110 of Nature Library volume on WILD FLOWERS.

Violet, White (See April)

Wake Robin, Large Flowered (See May)

JUNE

Willow-Herb, Great or Spiked Fire-weed

Flowering Season: June to September.
Parts of Country Where Found: Europe and Asia; Atlantic to Pacific, British Possessions to the Carolinas and Arizona.
Where to Look For: Dry soil, fields, roadsides, especially in burnt-over districts.
A full description of this brilliant flower is given on page 136 of Nature Library volume on WILD FLOWERS.

Wintergreen, Creeping; Checker- or Partridge-berry

Flowering Season: June to September.
Parts of Country Where Found: Newfoundland to Georgia, west to Michigan and Manitoba.
Where to Look For: Cool woods, especially under evergreens.
For a full description of this little plant, and its uses to bird, beast, and man, see page 159 of Nature Library volume on WILD FLOWERS.

Wood Sorrel, Violet (See May)

Wood Sorrel, White or True (See May)

Yarrow; Milfoil

Flowering Season: June to November.
Parts of Country Where Found: Naturalized from Europe and Asia through N. America.
Where to Look For: Waste land, dry fields, banks, roadsides.
This flower is described and an indication given of its part in mythology, medicine, folk-lore, and literature, on page 244 of Nature Library volume on WILD FLOWERS.

BUTTERFLIES TO BE WATCHED FOR IN JUNE

Swallowtail, Giant

A tropical species which is abundant throughout the Southern States. Now commonly found as far north as 42° latitude, from Nebraska eastward.
The butterflies of the first brood come from the chrysalids about the last of May and are found on the wing during June. The second brood come out about the last of July and are found on the wing during August and September.
For description of this butterfly, the life history of its caterpillar,

"the orange dog," the manner in which it repels birds, its insect enemies, etc., see page 62 of Nature Library volume on BUTTERFLIES.

Crescent, Silver

These butterflies appear on the wing during June and commonly disappear early in July. It is distributed over a large part of the United States, and a life history of the species, its caterpillar colonies, flowers with which the adults are associated, etc., will be found on page 141 of the Nature Library volume on BUTTERFLIES.

Skipper, Silver-spotted

These appear early in June in the Northern States and remain upon the wing for several weeks, being found even in August.
The species is widely distributed, occurring from ocean to ocean over nearly the whole of the United States. It extends into Canada only in the eastern part and is not found in the Northwestern States.
A full-color illustration of the butterfly appears in the Nature Library volume on BUTTERFLIES facing page 257, and a history of its life changes is given on page 270.

Blue, Scudder's

This butterfly is a northern species. It occurs in New England, New York, and Michigan, and thence extends far north into Canada. In New England there are two broods of the butterfly, one appearing early in June and the other late in July.
The caterpillar of this butterfly has a rather remarkable manner of feeding which is described, together with other interesting details, in an article on page 263 of the Nature Library volume on BUTTERFLIES.

Brown, the Eyed

This distinctly northern species has a rather limited range in Canada and New England. It extends south to Pennsylvania and Ohio and westward to Wisconsin and Iowa.
The butterflies emerge in June, and there is but one brood a year. The life history is given on page 221 of the Nature Library volume on BUTTERFLIES.

Emperor, the Gray

Found in the Southern States at least as far west as the Mississippi Valley; extends north to Indiana and Ohio.

JUNE

The caterpillars remain in a sort of stupor until the following spring. They become full-grown in May when they change to chrysalids, to emerge as the first brood of butterflies the following month.
A description of the life history of this Emperor, its associated plant, etc., will be found on page 210 of the Nature Library volume on BUTTERFLIES, and a full-color illustration appears facing page 209.

Emperor, the Goatweed

Comparatively few butterflies are confined so closely to the valley of the Mississippi River as the Goatweed Emperor. From southern Illinois south to the Gulf this insect is rather abundant in many localities where its food plant, the goatweed, is common.
It comes forth in spring and visits various spring and early summer flowers. Later the caterpillar makes a tent for itself by bending over and binding together the opposite margins of a leaf. On page 208 of the Nature Library volume on BUTTERFLIES a sketch of this detail appears, together with a description of the entire life history of the Goatweed Emperor. A full-color illustration is to be found on the page preceding the article.

Checker-spot, Harris'

Essentially a northern form, occurring only in a narrow strip of country east of Minnesota and Wisconsin running on the north through southern Canada and on the south through Michigan, New York, and Massachusetts.
The butterflies appear along roadsides and in open fields about the middle of June.
This insect, "one of the best-known botanists among all butterflies," is described on page 140 of the Nature Library volume on BUTTERFLIES.

Checker-spot, Baltimore

Is to be looked for only in peat bogs and swamps, and is present as a rule only from about the first of June to the middle of July. A full-color illustration to guide the collector will be found on page 160 of the Nature Library volume on BUTTERFLIES, and an article in which its life history is given will be found on page 135.

Fritillary, Mountain Silver-spot

This is preëminently a northern species, being especially abundant in the White Mountains of New Hampshire and ranging far northward into Canada and west through British America as far as the Mackenzie River.

The butterfly is single-brooded, laying the eggs on or near violets late in summer, the eggs hatching into larvæ that take no food until the following spring. They then begin to feed upon the violet leaves, become mature and change into chrysalids in time for the butterflies to emerge in June.

For a fuller description of the habits of this insect and means of identifying it at various stages of its life history, see page 126 of the Nature Library volume on BUTTERFLIES.

Monarch

June until October one may often see the stately Monarch flitting leisurely about over fields and meadows.

These butterflies come from the south in spring or early summer. They find milkweed plants and lay their eggs upon the leaves. These eggs soon hatch into small white and black caterpillars. One is likely to find them throughout most of the summer, wherever milkweed shows partially eaten leaves.

In early autumn these butterflies start southward on their long journey.

On page 233 of the Nature Library volume on BUTTERFLIES there is described the life changes of this familiar and interesting insect. Facing page 225 is a full-color illustration of the Monarch.

Azure—the Spring

Over the vast territory from Labrador across to Alaska and south to the Gulf of Mexico this little blue butterfly exists in so many different forms that it required special analytical keys to separate them.

Wherever these larvæ are found you will also find many ants wandering among them, and the moment the honey dew appears these ants begin to sip it up. This is by no means an isolated example of the relations between ants and other insects.

For description, habits, life changes, favorite food plants, etc., etc., see page 258 of Nature Library volume on BUTTERFLIES. For appearance in natural surroundings, identifying marks, etc., see full-color illustration opposite page 256.

Blue—the Silvery

The species occurs in the South Atlantic States, extending west as far as Wisconsin.

For description, habits, life changes, favorite food plants, etc., etc., see page 265 of Nature Library volume on BUTTERFLIES.
For appearance in natural surroundings, identifying marks, etc., see full-color illustration opposite page 257.

Blue—the Tailed

The species occurs clear to the Pacific Coast and ranges north and south over most of the northern continent.
For description, habits, life changes, favorite food plants, etc., etc., see page 264 of Nature Library volume on BUTTERFLIES.

Copper—the American

It commonly occurs from ocean to ocean, from the Hudson Bay region to the latitude of Georgia.
For description, habits, life changes, favorite food plants, etc., etc., see page 255 of Nature Library volume on BUTTERFLIES.

Copper—the Bronze

The Bronze Copper is a rare species, occurring from New England nearly to the Rocky Mountains.
For description, habits, life changes, favorite food plants, etc., etc., see page 257 of Nature Library volume on BUTTERFLIES.
For appearance in natural surroundings, identifying marks, etc., see full-color illustration opposite page 241.

Dog's-head Butterfly

Southern species which occasionally strays as far north as New York City, New Hampshire, Wisconsin, Iowa.
For description, habits, life changes, favorite food plants, etc., etc., see page 100 of Nature Library volume on BUTTERFLIES.
For appearance in natural surroundings, identifying marks, etc., see full-color illustration opposite page 112.

Fritillary—the White Mountain

Found only near the top of Mount Washington and other neighboring parts of the White Mountains.
For description, habits, life changes, favorite food plants, etc., etc., see page 127 of Nature Library volume on BUTTERFLIES.

Fritillary—the Variegated

A southern rather than a northern species, found occasionally from Montana to Massachusetts. In the more southern states

it is abundant and extends well through the continent of South America.
For description, habits, life changes, favorite food plants, etc., etc., see page 116 of Nature Library volume on BUTTERFLIES.

Fritillary—the Gulf

Has come north to our southern states, extending from ocean to ocean.
For description, habits, life changes, favorite food plants, etc., etc., see page 115 of Nature Library volume on BUTTERFLIES. For appearance in natural surroundings, identifying marks, etc., see full-color illustration opposite page 128.

Hair-streak—The Striped

Does not go far south, extending practically only to the southern borders of Kansas and Missouri.
For description, habits, life changes, favorite food plants, etc., etc., see page 247 of Nature Library volume on BUTTERFLIES.

Hair-streak—The White

This is also a southern species occurring at times as far north as Ohio and even Atlantic City, New Jersey.
It occurs as far north as West Virginia and Kentucky and ranges westward, at least to the Mississippi Valley.
For description, habits, life changes, favorite food plants, etc., etc., see page 244 of Nature Library volume on BUTTERFLIES.

Hair-streak—The Great Purple

A tropical form, extending into our southern borders from California to Florida and occasionally occurring north as far as southern Illinois.
For description, habits, life changes, favorite food plants, etc., etc., see page 243 of Nature Library volume on BUTTERFLIES. For appearance in natural surroundings, identifying marks, etc., see full-color illustration opposite page 241.

Orange-tip—The Olympian

In various parts of the Southern States.
For description, habits, life changes, favorite food plants, etc., etc., see page 96 of Nature Library volume on BUTTERFLIES.

JUNE

Papilio—The Short-tailed

Limited northern area in Newfoundland and around the Gulf of St. Lawrence—confined chiefly to this region.
For description, habits, life changes, favorite food plants, etc., etc., see page 75 of Nature Library volume on BUTTERFLIES.

Painted Beauty

This is a widely distributed butterfly, occurring from Canada to the Southern States and beyond.
For description, habits, life changes, favorite food plants, etc., etc., see page 163 of Nature Library volume on BUTTERFLIES.
For appearance in natural surroundings, identifying marks, etc., see full-color illustration opposite page 177.

Satyr—The Arctic

Normally an inhabitant of the Far North, extending around the North Pole over parts of three continents. Apparently, the only place in the United States where it occurs is a bog a little north of Bangor, Maine.
For description, habits, life changes, favorite food plants, etc., etc., see page 225 of Nature Library volume on BUTTERFLIES.

Skipper—The Least

The Least Skipper is one of the most widely distributed of all butterflies. It occurs from New England to Texas, south to Florida on the east coast, and west to the Rocky Mountains.
For description, habits, life changes, favorite food plants, etc., see page 281 of Nature Library volume on BUTTERFLIES.

Skipper—The Long-tailed

Distinctly a tropical species which is common along the Gulf Coast from Mexico to Florida. It ranges north along the Atlantic Coast to New York City and even to Connecticut.
For description, habits, life changes, favorite food plants, etc., etc., see page 271 of Nature Library volume on BUTTERFLIES.

Sulphur—Large Orange

Occurring in our extreme southern states and ranging occasionally as far north as Nebraska.
For description, habits, life changes, favorite food plants, etc., etc., see page 99 of Nature Library volume on BUTTERFLIES.

Sulphur—The Little

Essentially a southern species. Ranges from coast to coast and extends south into the tropics.
For description, habits, life changes, favorite food plants, etc., etc., see page 106 of Nature Library volume on BUTTERFLIES.

Sulphur—The Pink-edged

Characteristic northern species, occupying a rather narrow belt nearly along the fiftieth degree of latitude and extending west almost to the Pacific Coast.
For description, habits, life changes, favorite food plants, etc., etc., see page 104 of Nature Library volume on BUTTERFLIES.

Sulphur—The Orange

Essentially a tropical species. In the eastern United States it is rarely found north of latitude 40 degrees. Occurs from the Carolinas to Texas.
For description, habits, life changes, favorite food plants, etc., etc., see page 102 of Nature Library volume on BUTTERFLIES. For appearance in natural surroundings, identifying marks, etc., see full-color illustration opposite page 97.

Tortoise-shell—The American

The American Tortoise-shell is distinctly a northern species. North of latitude 43 degrees it seems to occur practically from ocean to ocean, extending far upward toward the Arctic region.
For description, habits, life changes, favorite food plants, etc., etc., see page 182 of Nature Library volume on BUTTERFLIES. For appearance in natural surroundings, identifying marks, etc., see full-color illustration facing page 193.

The Vicereine

In Florida and some of the other southern states.
For description, habits, life changes, favorite food plants, etc., etc., see page 206 of Nature Library volume on BUTTERFLIES.

The Wanderer

Widely distributed in eastern North America, occurring from Nova Scotia to Georgia and west to the Mississippi Valley.
For description, habits, life changes, favorite food plants, etc., etc., see page 253 of Nature Library volume on BUTTERFLIES.

JUNE

White—The Great Southern

The species is distinctly tropical, extending northward into our Southern States.
For description, habits, life changes, favorite food plants, etc., etc., see page 90 of Nature Library volume on BUTTERFLIES.

Wood-nymph—The Southern

Abundant in the extreme Southern States and has occasionally been taken much farther north.
For description habits, life changes, favorite food plants, etc., etc., see page 218 of Nature Library volume on BUTTERFLIES.

Zebra Butterfly

The zebra butterfly belongs to one of these tropical tribes.
Found commonly only in Florida and one or two other neighboring states.
For description, habits, life changes, favorite food plants, etc., etc., see page 229 of Nature Library volume on BUTTERFLIES.
For appearance in natural surroundings, identifying marks, etc., see full-color illustration opposite page 225.

TREES TO BE WATCHED IN JUNE

The American Beech

The delicate flowers of the beech tree are rarely seen; they fade so soon. The stamen tassels drop off and the forming nuts, with their prickly burs, are more and more in evidence in the leaf angles near the ends of the new shoots.
A full description of this tree, its leafage, flowers, and fruit, its seeding, its uses, etc., will be found on page 42 of the Nature Library volume on TREES.

The Honey Locust

Its fern-like feathery aspect is the tree's greatest charm in early June. A full-color illustration to aid in its identification will be found on page 180 of the Nature Library volume on TREES, preceded by an article describing its manner of growth, the process of seeding, the interesting phases of its spring, summer, and autumn cycle, with its uses to man, etc.

Great Laurel; Rose Bay

The evergreen leaves and the buds, full of promise for June blossoming, are the beautiful features of this rhododendron and others in winter.

The distribution of this tree, with a description of its distinguishing features, leafage, bloom, etc., will be found on page 119 of the Nature Library volume on TREES.

Mountain Laurel

In June and July the polished evergreen foliage of the kalmia bushes is almost overwhelmed by the masses of its exquisite pink blossoms.

For a description of this bush, with the curious contrivance in its flower to insure cross-fertilization through the help of bees, see page 120 of the Nature Library volume on TREES.

ANIMALS TO BE NOTED IN JUNE

American Prong-Horn

The white area on each buttock serves the antelope in unusual fashion.

A musk gland concealed in the centre of the patch produces scent that can be distinguished by the antelope at great distance.

The fawns are commonly two in number, born in late May or early June.

In September the antelope bands offer at times a pretty picture in their community gambols that are probably unique in the animal world.

Description, range, habits of mating, food-getting and shelter, etc., will be found on page 37 of the Nature Library volume on ANIMALS.

Franklin Ground-squirrel

The young are born about the middle of May. By the end of June, they are a third grown, and by September they are not to be distinguished from their parents either in activity or appearance. Appearance, markings that are characteristic, range, home localities, with other interesting details, are to be found on page 79 of Nature Library volume on ANIMALS.

JULY, The Thunder Moon

In July the year is full grown, lusty. In May the wild plants along the edge of the brook through the fields were only a fringe a few inches high; now some of them are waist-high, even shoulder-high—forming a hedge that must be pushed aside to reach the water. Here are turtle-head, joe-pye-weed, jewel-weed, the budding golden rods, and the rasping smartweed. Do you know them all by sight? You may feel the quick sting of a nettle, too, seen too late. And in the woods and the roadside thickets it will be well to take care, or you may have cause to regret the touch of "poison ivy" or poison sumach.

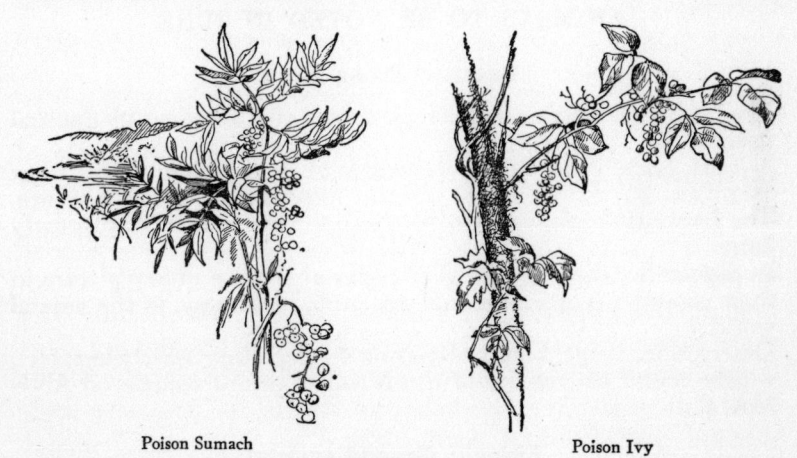

Poison Sumach   Poison Ivy

Do you know how to tell it at a glance from the harmless Virginia creeper? An ounce of preventive information would have saved many a picnicker a most painful experience. The simple difference between the harmful and the harmless is a lesson in botany which every walker in the country should hasten to learn.

We cannot do better than memorize the four points of identification given by William Hamilton Gibson:

First: The poison ivy, or sumach, has *three* leaves.
Second: The five-leaved is harmless.
Third: The poison sumachs have *white* berries.
Fourth: No *red-berried* sumach is poisonous.

And if you have difficulty in remembering "which is which" this little jingle, also from Mr. Gibson, will be a help to you on your walks in the fields and woods.

"Berries red,
Have no dread!
Berries white
Poisonous sight!
Leaves three,
Quickly flee!"

Virginia Creeper (Harmless)

In July, the true aim of all the spring outburst of greenery and blossoms becomes apparent. Look at the branches of the dogwood tree that was a mass of white in May, and you will find the little green seed vessels. Look among the leaves of last April's violet bed at the edge of the thicket, and you will find tiny pods filled with hard little seeds. Look at your trousers or golf stockings when you come home from your walks and you will have to pick out the burrs and the little barbed and hooked seeds, the "seed tramps" which have stolen a ride with you, hoping to be dropped again upon ground far from where they grew. Even now, in July, the "high moon of the year," Nature is looking ahead and preparing for next spring. It would be interesting to spend one of your Sunday strolls this month in looking for the seed vessels of the spring

JULY

flowers that are gone, and in trying to name the plants without their blossoms.

Nature always holds surprises in store for us, but no matter how startling they are, there is always a reason for them. Sometime you will stop suddenly at the sight of a dried snake skin hanging, it may be, from a hole in some old apple tree! How did it get there? After you have read a particular page in your Nature Library volume on BIRDS you will know that the snake skin didn't get there by accident. It was brought there by the Great Crested Flycatcher. His nest is never without a snake's discarded clothes, if he can find a suit of them anywhere in the neighborhood, and he usually can. Sometimes there are three or four. This habit of collecting snake skins for nest decoration is so characteristic that this Flycatcher has been called "the snake specialist." Does he use them to frighten away enemies? That is the usual explanation—but no one knows.

Crested Flycatcher

You should try, this summer, to find a hummingbird's nest. If you succeed, you will be entitled to pat yourself on the back, for it is as rare and difficult a thing to find as any single thing you can go out looking for. When completed it is scarcely larger than an English walnut, and it takes a keen eye to distinguish it from a knot on the limb of the tree where it hides. You will come upon one now and then, but not many in a whole lifetime. If you do find one, it will probably come as a "surprise," when you are looking for something else.

But here is a "surprise" that you *can* look for and probably find any time during the late summer. If you come upon a sassafras bush, you will want to dig out a bit of the fragrant, delicious root to chew for its spicy flavor. When you have done this, look over the bush for folded leaves. When you have found one, pry the folds apart gently with a twig and look within.

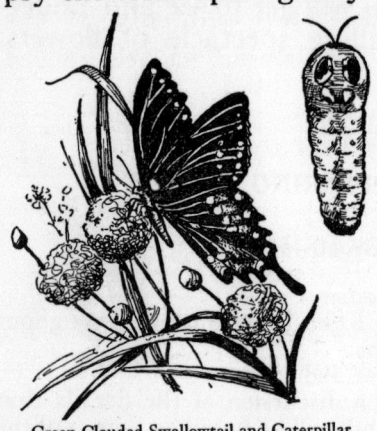

As you do so, you may be startled, and drop the folded leaf hurriedly, for two of the queerest staring "eyes" you ever saw will peep out at you. If you look closer, however, you will see that the two spots are not real eyes at all, but merely "eye spots" on the back of a caterpillar who lives upon the sassafras and makes a home for itself by folding over a leaf.

Green Clouded Swallowtail and Caterpillar

This is an example of the "terrifying devices" which Nature gives to some of the weakest creatures, in order that they may frighten away their enemies. The unwinking stare of those two make-believe eyes, seen suddenly, might disconcert even a hungry bird intent upon finding a caterpillar dinner.

If you take home the sassafras caterpillar, with some of the bush's leaves for food, he will finally come out as a beautiful butterfly, called the "Green Clouded Swallowtail," but it may not happen until next spring.

July is a time of profusion and plenty among Nature's wonders. Dozens of other butterflies are upon the wing. You ought to try to identify at least a few—the mourning cloak; the big red-brown milkweed butterfly; the big yellow tiger swallowtail; the small yellow cabbage butterfly; the painted beauty; the red admiral; the common wood-nymph; the black swallowtail; the red-spotted purple, and the viceroy.

The trouble with summer is that there is too much of

JULY

it while it lasts. The various volumes of your Nature Library will give you more fascinating things to observe than you are likely to have time for in the spare time of only one season. But next year you can do more, and each time summer comes you will get to see and understand still more of its thrilling spectacle of flowers, birds, trees, and insects.

WILD FLOWERS APPEARING IN JULY

Arrow-head, Broad-leaved

Flowering Season: July to September.
Parts of Country Where Found: From Mexico north throughout our area to the circumpolar regions.
Where to Look For: Shallow water and mud.
A description of this plant, with a discussion of the details that enable it to live in water and on land, will be found on page 3 of the Nature Library volume on WILD FLOWERS.

Aster, Red-stalked, Purple-stemmed, or Early Purple

Flowering Season: July to November.
Where to Look For: "Even wetter ground" than the New England aster.
This flower is described on page 231 of the Nature Library volume on WILD FLOWERS.

Beard-Tongue, Hairy (See May)
Bellflower, Clasping; Venus' Looking Glass (See May)
Bergamot, Wild (See June)
Bindweed, Hedge or Great Wild Morning Glory (See June)
Black-eyed Susan; Yellow or Ox-eyed Daisy (See May)
Bluets (See April)
Blue-eyed Grass, Pointed (See May)
Bouncing Bet; Soapwort (See June)

NATURE'S PROGRAM

Boneset; Thoroughwort

Flowering Season: July to September.
Parts of Country Where Found: From Gulf States north to Nebraska, New Brunswick, and Manitoba.
Where to Look For: Wet ground, low meadows, roadsides.
A description of this flower, with an account of its many insect visitors, is to be found on page 225 of Nature Library volume on WILD FLOWERS.

Brooklime (See April)

Bunchberry; Low or Dwarf Cornel (See May)

Bugloss, Viper's; Blue Weed; Blue Thistle or Devil (See June)

Buttercup, Common Meadow; Tall Crowfoot (see May)

Buttercup, Swamp (See April)

Butterfly Weed; Orange Milkweed (See June)

Button-bush; Honey-balls; Button-ball Shrub (See June)

Calapogon; Grass Pink (See June)

Camomile, Dog's or Fetid

Flowering Season: June to November.
Parts of Country Where Found: Throughout North America, except in circumpolar regions.
Where to Look For: Roadsides, dry waste land, sandy fields.
Description and identifying characteristics to be found on page 245 of Nature Library volume on WILD FLOWERS.

Campion, Starry (See June)

Celandine (See April)

Carrot, Wild; Queen Anne's Lace (See June)

Chicory; Succory

Flowering Season: July to October.
Parts of Country Where Found: Common in eastern U. S. and Canada, south to the Carolinas; also sparingly west to Nebraska.
Where to Look For: Roadsides, waste places, fields.
A description of this familiar little flower, with its uses, etc., is given on page 252 of Nature Library volume on WILD FLOWERS. A full-color illustration appears facing page 241.

JULY

Clover, Yellow Sweet; Yellow Melilot (See June)
Clover, White or Dutch (See May)
Clover, White Sweet; White Melilot (See June)
Cohosh, Black, or Black Snakeroot (See June)
Corn Cockle; Corn Rose; Corn or Red Campion

Flowering Season: July to September.
Parts of Country Where Found: United States at large, especially Central and Western States. Europe and Asia.
Where to Look For: Wheat and other grain fields; dry, waste places.
For description of this flower see page 49 Nature Library volume on WILD FLOWERS.

Culver's Root or Physic (See June)
Dayflower, Virginia or Common (See June)
Dodder, Gronovius' or Common

Flowering Season: July to September.
Parts of Country Where Found: Nova Scotia and Manitoba to the Gulf States.
Where to Look For: Moist soil, meadows, ditches, beside streams. This plant, called often "Strangle-weed," is no honest one, but a parasite, whose ways of growth are described in article on page 179 of Nature Library volume on WILD FLOWERS.

Dogbane, Spreading, or Flytrap (See June)
Dogwood, Swamp; Silky Cornel (See May)
Elecampane; Horseheal; Yellow Starwort

Flowering Season: July to September.
Parts of Country Where Found: Nova Scotia and the Carolinas to Minnesota and Missouri.
Where to Look For: Roadsides, fields, fence rows, damp pastures. Described on page 239 of Nature Library volume on WILD FLOWERS.

Everlasting, Pearly or Large-flowered

Flowering Season: July to September.
Parts of Country Where Found: North Carolina, Kansas, and California far north.

Where to Look For: Dry fields, hillsides, open woods, uplands. The interesting mechanism for fertilization of this flower is described on page 238 of Nature Library volume on WILD FLOWERS.

Fleabane, Daisy; Sweet Scabious (See May)

Forget-Me-Not (See May)

Foxglove, Downy False

Flowering Season: July to August.
Parts of Country Where Found: Eastern Massachusetts to Ontario and Wisconsin, south to southern New York, Georgia, and Mississippi.
Where to Look For: Gravelly or sandy soil, dry thickets, open woods.
A description of this flower is to be found on page 207 of Nature Library volume on WILD FLOWERS, and a full-color illustration showing appearance in its natural surroundings is facing page 193.

Frostweed, Hoary (See June)

Frostweed, Long-branched; Frost Flower, or Frostwort; Canadian Rock Rose (See May)

Gold Thread; Canker Root (See May)

Golden-Rod, Early, Plum, or Sharp-toothed (See June)

Golden-Rod, Gray or Field

Flowering Season: July to November.
Parts of Country Where Found: Quebec and Northwest Territory to Gulf States.
Where to Look For: Open, sterile places.
This most brilliantly colored of the golden-rods is described on page 229 of Nature Library volume on WILD FLOWERS.

Golden-Rod, Sweet

Flowering Season: July to September.
Parts of Country Where Found: New England to Gulf States.
Where to Look For: Dry soil.
Means of identifying this golden-rod amongst the many of its tribe are described on page 228 of Nature Library volume on WILD FLOWERS.

JULY

Golden-Rod, White; Silver-Rod

Flowering Season: July to September.
Parts of Country Where Found: New Brunswick and Georgia to beyond the Mississippi.
Where to Look For: Dry soil.
This plant approaches more nearly the idea of a rod than its fellows. It is described on page 227 of Nature Library volume on WILD FLOWERS.

Golden-Rod, Wrinkle-leaved, or Tall, or Hairy

Flowering Season: July to November.
Parts of Country Where Found: Newfoundland and Ontario to Gulf States.
Where to Look For: Dry soil.
This "perversely variable species" of golden-rod is described on page 228 of the Nature Library volume on WILD FLOWERS.

Golden-Rod, Zig-zag, or Broad-leaved

Flowering Season: July to September.
Parts of Country Where Found: New Brunswick and Georgia to beyond the Mississippi.
Where to Look For: Rich woodlands and thicket borders.
This woodland golden-rod is described on page 227 of the Nature Library volume on WILD FLOWERS.

Ground-nut

Flowering Season: July to September.
Parts of Country Where Found: New Brunswick and Ontario to the Gulf States and Kansas.
Where to Look For: Twining about undergrowth and thickets in moist or wet ground.
This little flower, with its edible root-stock, is described on page 112 of the Nature Library volume on WILD FLOWERS.

Hardhack; Steeple Bush

Flowering Season: July to September.
Parts of Country Where Found: Nova Scotia westward, south to Georgia and Kansas.
Where to Look For: Low, moist grounds, roadside ditches, swamps.
On the leaves of this little plant, with its pretty pink spires, why are the undersides so woolly? See the description on page 94 of the Nature Library volume on WILD FLOWERS.

NATURE'S PROGRAM

Harebell or Hairbell (See June)

Hawkweed, Orange or Tawny (See June)

Hellebore, American White; Indian Poke (See May)

Herb Robert (See May)

Indian Pipe; Ice Plant; Ghost Flower; Corpse Plant (See June)

Indian Pipe (See June)

Indigo, Wild; Yellow or Indigo Broom (See June)

Iris, Blue; Larger Blue Flag; Fleur-de-Lis (See May)

Iron-weed

Flowering Season: July to September.
Parts of Country Where Found: Massachusetts to Georgia, west to the Mississippi.
Where to Look For: Moist soil, meadows, fields.
This flower, sometimes mistaken for an aster, will be found described on page 222 of the Nature Library volume on WILD FLOWERS.

Jamestown Weed; Jimson Weed; Thorn Apple (See June)

Jewel-weed; Spotted Touch-me-not; Snap Weed

Flowering Season: July to October.
Parts of Country Where Found: Nova Scotia and Oregon to Missouri and Florida.
Where to Look For: Beside streams, ponds, ditches, moist ground.
The jewel-weed with its tiny "horn of plenty" for the humming-bird and other lovers of its nectar, is described on page 124 of Nature Library volume of WILD FLOWERS.

Lady's Slipper, Large Yellow; Yellow Moccasin Flower (See May)

Lady's Slipper, Small Yellow (See May)

Ladies' Tresses, Nodding

Flowering Season: July to October.
Parts of Country Where Found: Nova Scotia to the Gulf of Mexico; west to the Mississippi.
Where to Look For: Low meadows, ditches, and swamps.

JULY

The flowers of this little orchid are marvellous pieces of mechanism, to which men like Darwin have devoted hours of study. Ladies' Tresses are described on page 43 of the Nature Library volume on WILD FLOWERS.

Laurel, Sheep; Narrow-leaved Laurel (See June)
Lettuce, Tall or Wild; Horseweed (See June)
Lily, Blackberry (See June)
Lily, Red, Wood, or Flame (See June)
Lily, Sweet-Scented White Water; Pond Lily (See June)
Lily, Turk's Cap

Flowering Season: July and August.
Parts of Country Where Found: New Brunswick to Minnesota and southward.
Where to Look For: Low meadows and marshes; rich soil.
Tallest and most prolific of bloom among our lilies, as it is the most variable in color, size and form. Described on page 15 of Nature Library volume on WILD FLOWERS.

Lily, Wild Yellow, Meadow, Field or Canada (See June)
Lobelia, Great; Blue Cardinal Flower

Flowering Season: July to October.
Parts of Country Where Found: Ontario and northern U. S., west to Dakota, south to Kansas and Georgia.
Where to Look For: Moist or wet soil; beside streams.
Described on page 221 of Nature Library volume on WILD FLOWERS.

Lobelia, Red; Cardinal Flower

Flowering Season: July to September.
Parts of Country Where Found: New Brunswick to the Gulf States, west to Kansas and Northwest Territory.
Where to Look For: Wet or low ground, beside streams, ditches, and meadow runnels.
This flower entices the humming-bird, as do all flowers of its hue. See page 220 of Nature Library volume on WILD FLOWERS for description.

Loosestrife, Four-leaved or Whorled (See June)
Lupine, Wild; Wild Pea (See May)

Meadow-rue, Tall

Flowering Season: July to September.
Parts of Country Where Found: Quebec to Florida, west to Ohio.
Where to Look For: Open, sunny swamps, beside sluggish water; low meadows.
These flowers possess an "unseasonable, ethereal, chaste, springlike beauty." They are what botanists term polygamous flowers. Described on page 59 of Nature Library volume on WILD FLOWERS.

Meadow-Sweet (See June)

Milkweed, Common; Common Silkweed (See June)

Milkwort, Common, Field or Purple; Purple Polygala (See June)

Milkwort, Fringed; Polygala (See May)

Monkey Flower (See June)

Motherwort (See June)

Mullein, Great; Velvet or Flannel Plant; Mullein Dock (See June)

Mullein, Moth (See June)

Mustard, Black (See June)

Mustard, Field or Corn (See May)

Mustard, Hedge (See May)

New Jersey Tea (See May)

Nightshade; Bittersweet; Blue Bindweed (See May)

Orchis, Large, or Early, Purple-fringed (See June)

Orchis, White-fringed

Flowering Season: July to August.
Parts of Country Where Found: Northeastern United States and eastern Canada to Newfoundland.
Where to Look For: Peat bogs and swamps.
"Not for man, but for the bee, the moth and the butterfly, are orchids where they are and what they are." See page 39 of Nature Library volume on WILD FLOWERS for description of the white-fringed orchis.

Orchis, Yellow-fringed

Flowering Season: July to August.
Parts of Country Where Found: Vermont and Ontario to Florida and Texas.

JULY   107

Where to look for: Moist meadows and sandy bogs.
For description see page 40 of the Nature Library volume on WILD FLOWERS.

Oswego Tea; Bee Balm

Flowering Season: July to September.
Parts of Country Where Found: Canada to Georgia, west to Michigan.
Where to Look For: Moist soil, especially near streams, in hilly or mountainous regions.
This flower, brightening the landscape, is host to bumblebees, butterflies, and humming-birds, who feast on its store of nectar. Described on page 190 of Nature Library volume on WILD FLOWERS. Full-color illustration faces page 177.

Painted Cup, Scarlet; Indian Paint Brush (See May)

Parnassus, Grass of

Flowering Season: July to September.
Parts of Country Where Found: New Brunswick to Virginia, west to Iowa.
Where to Look For: Wet ground, low meadows, swamps.
Described on page 92 of Nature Library volume on WILD FLOWERS.

Parsnip, Wild or Field (See June)

Persicaria, Common; Pink Knotweed, or Jointweed, or Smartweed

Flowering Season: July to October.
Parts of Country Where Found: Nova Scotia and Minnesota to the Gulf and Texas.
Where to Look For: Waste places, roadsides, moist soil.
This little flower, which attracts many insects, is described on page 46 of Nature Library volume on WILD FLOWERS.

Pickerel Weed (See June)

Pimpernel, Scarlet; Red Chickweed; Poor Man's or Shepherd's Weatherglass or Clock (See May)

Pine Sap; False Beech Drops (See June)

Pink, Rose; Bitter-bloom; Square-stemmed Sabbatia

Flowering Season: July to August.
Parts of Country Where Found: New York and Florida to Ontario, Michigan, and Oklahoma.

Where to Look For: Rich soil, meadows, thickets.
Much sought by herb gatherers for use as a tonic medicine, else it would be much commoner than it is. Description on page 165 of Nature Library volume on WILD FLOWERS.

Pink, Swamp; Swamp Honeysuckle; White or Clammy Azalea
(See June)

Pink, Sea or Marsh

Flowering Season: July to September.
Parts of Country Where Found: Maine to Florida; more rarely, Gulf shores to Louisiana.
Where to Look For: Salt meadows and marshes, borders of brackish rivers; rarely in the sand at the edges of fresh-water ponds a little way inland.
This lovely flower, with a yellow eye rimmed with carmine, is described on page 166 of the Nature Library volume on WILD FLOWERS.

Pipsissewa; Prince's Pine (See June)
Poke Weed; Scoke; Pigeon-berry; Ink-berry; Garget (See June)
Primrose, Evening (See June)
Rattlesnake Weed; Early or Vein-leaf Hawkweed (See May)
Raspberry, Purple-flowering or Virginia (See June)
Rhododendron, American or Great; Great Laurel (See June)
Rose, Smoother, Early, or Meadow (See June)
Rose, Swamp (See May)
Saint John's-wort, Common (See June)

Saint John's-wort, Great or Giant

Flowering Season: Midsummer.
Parts of Country Where Found: North of New Jersey and westward to Iowa.
Where to Look For: Banks of streams.
Described on page 131 of Nature Library volume on WILD FLOWERS.

Saint John's-wort, Shrubby

Flowering season: July to September.
Parts of Country Where Found: New Jersey southward.

JULY

Where to Look For: Sandy or rocky places.
Description to be found on page 130 of Nature Library volume on WILD FLOWERS.

Self-Heal; Heal-All (See May)

Senna, Wild or American

Flowering Season: July and August.
Parts of Country Where Found: New England west to Nebraska and south to the Gulf States.
Where to Look For: Alluvial or moist, rich soil, swamps, roadsides.
Caterpillars of several sulphur butterflies feed on this plant. For description see page 103 of Nature Library volume on WILD FLOWERS.

Shepherd's Purse; Mother's Heart

Flowering Season: Almost throughout the year.
Parts of Country Where Found: Over nearly all parts of the earth.
Where to Look For: Fields, roadsides, waste places.
From Europe this little low plant found its way, to become the commonest of our weeds, so completing its march around the globe. What is the secret of its successful march over the face of the earth? Described on page 81 of the Nature Library volume on WILD FLOWERS.

Skullcap, Larger or Hyssop (See May)

Skullcap, Mad-dog; Helmet-flower; Hoodwort

Flowering Season: July to September.
Parts of Country Where Found: Uneven throughout the U. S. and British Possessions
Where to Look For: Wet, shady ground.
Flower, leaf, and fruit of this little plant are described on page 187 of Nature Library volume on WILD FLOWERS.

Speedwell, Common (See May)

Spikenard; Indian Root; Spignet

Flowering Season: July and August.
Parts of Country Where Found: New Brunswick and Georgia to the Mississippi.
Where to Look For: Rich, open woods, wayside thickets, light soil.
A striking, decorative plant, once upon a time much sought after

for its medicinal properties. Described on page 139 of Nature Library volume on WILD FLOWERS.

Spikenard, Wild False Solomon's Seal (See May)
Star-Grass, Yellow (See May)
Sundew, Round-leaved

Flowering Season: July and August.
Parts of Country Where Found: Labrador and the Gulf to Alaska and California; Europe and Asia.
Where to Look For: Bogs, sandy and sunny marshes.
Nothing could be more innocent-looking than this tiny plant, yet, according to the account on page 87 of the Nature Library volume on WILD FLOWERS, it is a "bloodthirsty little miscreant," over whose mechanism Darwin and other naturalists have spent hours and hours of study.

Sweetbrier; Eglantine (See June)
Tansy; Bitter-buttons

Flowering Season: July to September.
Parts of Country Where Found: Naturalized from Europe; Nova Scotia and Minnesota to Missouri and North Carolina.
Where to Look For: Roadsides; commonly escaped from gardens.
A description of this flower, with interesting accounts of the traditions with which it is associated, and its old-time uses, is given on page 249 of Nature Library volume on WILD FLOWERS.

Thistle, Common, or Plumed, or Bull

Flowering Season: July to November.
Parts of Country Where Found: Native to Europe and Asia; naturalized from Newfoundland to Georgia, west to Nebraska.
Where to Look For: Fields, pastures.
A full-color illustration of this thistle faces page 240 of the Nature Library volume on WILD FLOWERS. A description of this flower, upon whose seed the gold-finch feeds, and over which bees and butterflies may be seen hovering the world over, will be found on page 250.

Thistle, Pasture or Fragrant

Flowering Season: July to September.
Parts of Country Where Found: Maine to Delaware.
Where to Look For: Fields, pastures.

JULY

The fascinating account of thistles beginning on page 250 of the Nature Library volume on WILD FLOWERS includes a special paragraph on this flower on page 252.

Toadflax, Blue or Wild; Linaria (See May)

Touch-me-not, Pale

Flowering Season: July to October.
Parts of Country Where Found: Most abundant northward in same range as jewel weed.
Where to Look For: Beside streams, ponds, ditches; moist grounds.
This plant shares the popular names of jewel-weed and is described on page 126 of Nature Library volume on WILD FLOWERS.

Turtle-head; Snake- or Cod-head

Flowering Season: July to September.
Parts of Country Where Found: Newfoundland to Florida, and halfway across the continent.
Where to Look For: Ditches, beside streams, swamps.
A fascinating account of the relation between bumblebee and turtle-head is given on page 202 of the Nature Library volume on WILD FLOWERS, where this flower is fully described.

Vervain, Blue; Wild Hyssop (See June)

Vetch, Blue, Tufted, or Cow; Tare (See June)

Virgin's Bower; Virginia Clematis

Flowering Season: July to September.
Parts of Country Where Found: Georgia and Kansas northward; less common in Canada.
Where to Look For: Climbing over woodland borders, thickets, roadside shrubbery, fences, and walls; rich, moist soil.
A full-page colored illustration precedes the description on page 65 of Nature Library volume on WILD FLOWERS, in which Darwin's discovery in regard to the clematis leaf and other interesting facts are given.

Willow Herb, Great or Spiked Fireweed (See June)
Wintergreen, Creeping; Checker- or Partridge-berry (See June)
Wood Sorrel, White or True (See May)
Yarrow; Milfoil (See June)

BUTTERFLIES TO BE WATCHED FOR IN JULY

The Buckeye

The Buckeye has an extraordinary range, being found from Cuba to Massachusetts and from the Atlantic to the Pacific coasts. Toward the northern limits of its range it is very rare and one of the greatest prizes which the collector can obtain.

In our Southern States it is an abundant and generally distributed butterfly, and, as it hibernates as an adult and one group follows another through the season rather rapidly, it is likely to be taken at almost any time.

In the Nature Library volume on BUTTERFLIES on page 188 will be found noted the identifying characteristics of this prized specimen. Find out from this article which food plants to watch in the fields and woods for the tiny eggs which the mother Buckeye lays, one at a time. Facing page 193 is a full-color illustration of this butterfly.

Comma, The Gray

In what hidden places do these butterflies sleep throughout the winter; in spring awakening to lay their eggs singly on leaves of currants, gooseberries, and related plants?,

A summer brood of young butterflies appears in July, and another brood in August or September.

An article on the Gray Comma appears on page 158 of Nature Library volume on BUTTERFLIES, with an identifying full-color illustration opposite page 177.

Crescent, the Pearl

Occurs over practically the whole of the United States and Canada and is found from early spring until late in autumn.

When you see a butterfly flying leisurely from plant to plant and alighting upon leaves rather than on blossoms, you may be pretty sure she is bent upon egg-laying. Do you know that the mother Pearl Crescent has been called "a better botanist than most of us" by one of the most distinguished American naturalists? And do you know why?

The Pearl Crescent is described on page 143 of Nature Library volume on BUTTERFLIES and a full-color illustration is to be found facing page 161.

Dusky-wing, the Sleepy

These butterflies are to be found in early summer. Look for them hovering above blueberry bushes.

JULY

Described on page 275 of Nature Library volume on BUTTERFLIES.

Emperor, the Tawny

This is a southern species, found more or less abundantly from southern New York to northern Florida and across the country to a line drawn from Iowa to Texas.

Clusters of from two to five hundred eggs may be found on the leaves of hackberry sometime in July. The caterpillars emerge a week later in a curiously interesting way.

Description of the Tawny Emperor is to be found on page 212 of Nature Library volume on BUTTERFLIES, and a full-color illustration faces page 224.

Fritillary, the Great Spangled

These butterflies mature late in June or early in July and remain alive until early September. The mother remains upon the wing through many weeks, so that toward the end of August or early September a large proportion of the specimens have a decidedly frayed appearance. Why does the mother wait so long before laying her eggs?

A full-color illustration of the Great Spangled Fritillary appears opposite page 145 of Nature Library volume on BUTTERFLIES as a help in identifying this insect, and an article describing its life changes is found on page 122.

Fritillary, the Regal

To be found almost any time during July, August, and September, in a belt of territory running from New England and the Atlantic States westward at least to Nebraska.

Late in June or early in July the adults are released from the chrysalis. They continue to come forth for several weeks, apparently until nearly the middle of August. An interesting point for some young observer to determine is how this butterfly lays her eggs. This point is discussed in the article on page 120 of the Nature Library volume on BUTTERFLIES, and a full-color illustration faces page 144.

Fritillary, The Silver-spot

Widely distributed over southern Canada and the Northern States. It extends south to Virginia and Pennsylvania and west to Nebraska, Montana, and Washington.

The Silver-spots are on the wing for several weeks in summer.

During the latter part of this time, the females lay eggs upon violet leaves.
Described on page 125 of Nature Library volume on BUTTERFLIES, with full-color illustration facing page 145.

Hair-streak, the Acadian

Here is an opportunity for some young observer to make a real contribution to science, for so far as is known to scientists, the eggs of this butterfly and the situation in which they are laid have never been described.
Found from New Zealand west to Montana along a rather restricted area, which coincides pretty closely with the southern part of the Transition Zone.
These butterflies appear during July and August.
A description of the Acadian Hair-streak will be found on page 248 of Nature Library volume on BUTTERFLIES.

Hair-streak, the Banded

This butterfly offers another opportunity for young nature students to send in original observations. Information as to the habits of the young caterpillars of this species is still uncertain, although it is known that the mother prefers to lay her tiny green eggs upon the leaves of certain favored trees.
The Banded Hair-streak is described on page 246 of the Nature Library volume on BUTTERFLIES and its known habits recorded there.

Hair-streak, the Gray

Ranges from New Hampshire to Florida and Central America, but apparently occurs only rarely north of the United States.
The butterflies are found upon the wing almost any time in summer, especially from early June until late in August.
Their curious little caterpillars, with "extensile heads" adapted to feed upon the fruits or seed-pods of its various food plants, are described in the article giving life history on page 245 of Nature Library volume on BUTTERFLIES. Full-color illustration faces page 241.

The Pearly Eye

One of the rarest of American butterflies, distinctly a woodland species, being found only in little glades in the midst of woods and apparently seldom even seeking flowers for their nectar.
It may be looked for in woodland glens in all parts of the United

JULY

States east of the western limits of the Mississippi Valley and south of Canada, except perhaps the lower part of Florida.
Adults appear shortly before midsummer and continue on the wing through July and at least part of August. See page 219 of the Nature Library volume on BUTTERFLIES for characteristics of especial interest peculiar to Pearly Eyes.

Purple, the Banded

This butterfly, with its striking color markings (shown on page 208 of Nature Library volume on BUTTERFLIES), is a northern form, ranging to a large extent north of the regions occupied by the Viceroy, the caterpillars of both having the same curious habits and bearing a close resemblance to each other.
The Banded Purple butterflies appear in June and lay their eggs in July upon the tips of the leaves of birches, especially the black birch, coming out about the middle of the following May when the spring warmth starts the buds of its food plant.
The Banded Purple is described on page 202 of the Nature Library volume on BUTTERFLIES.

The Viceroy

Found over a large part of North America, flying freely from June until autumn over meadows, fields, and open glades.
"The larvæ of the autumnal brood," wrote Dr. Riley, "when about one fourth or one third grown, build for themselves curious little houses in which they pass the winter . . . commonly found upon our willows and poplars in the winter time . . . nearly always made so near the ground that they are protected by snow during most of the winter."
Facing page 193 of the Nature Library volume on BUTTERFLIES will be found a full-color illustration of the adult Viceroy, and from pages 195 to 202 there appears a long account of the fascinating life changes and habits of this insect.

Purple, the Red-spotted

The adults appear in early summer and lay eggs which develop into butterflies again during the latter part of the summer. The favorite food plants of the larvæ are among the great order to which belong the apple, pear, cherry, rose, and many other common trees and shrubs.
The protective devices found upon the tiny eggs do not always prevent their attack by tiny parasites, and probably many others are eaten by ants and spiders. Do you know what these devices are?

The Red-spotted Purple is described on page 204 of the Nature Library volume on BUTTERFLIES, and a full-color illustration appears facing page 209.

Sulphur, the Brimstone or Cloudless

Coming as migrants from the south, singly or in scattered flocks in early summer, they fly north to New England, Wisconsin, and Nebraska. The precise conditions, however, under which they lay their eggs, are not well known, and need careful observations in various localities.

Other interesting facts in regard to the Cloudless Sulphur are found in an article on page 98 of the Nature Library volume on BUTTERFLIES.

Sulphur, the Clouded

This is about the only medium-sized yellow butterfly generally found in the Northeastern States. The adults may be seen from spring until autumn. They lay their eggs upon clover and other plants, and the small green caterpillars are so protectively colored that they are seen comparatively seldom upon the leaves.

This charming summer visitor, a favorite with New England authors, is described on page 101 of Nature Library volume on BUTTERFLIES. A full-color illustration will be found facing page 113.

Swallowtail, the Blue

This is a southern species, found from the Carolinas to California, but occasionally occurs as far north as New England. Young observers can be helpful to scientists in finding out more about this species of the Swallowtails. In what way, can be learned by reading the article on this insect which appears on page 65 of the Nature Library volume on BUTTERFLIES. A picture in full color follows page 64.

White, the Checkered or Cabbage Butterfly

This familiar butterfly has two fairly distinct forms, the spring form and the summer form.

It has some very interesting sleeping habits. These with other important facts are related in an article on page 88 of the Nature Library volume on BUTTERFLIES. A full-color illustration appears facing page 81.

JULY

The White Mountain Butterfly

To appreciate the extraordinary distribution of this notable butterfly one must let his fancy carry him back a million years or so until he reaches that old time when the northern part of the American continent was covered with an icy coating.
Of this, and of the life history and habits of this remarkable insect, read the article which begins on page 222 of the Nature Library volume on BUTTERFLIES.

Wood-nymph, the Common or Blue-eyed Grayling

During recent years many collectors have gathered these butterflies from all parts of North America. They emerge during July and August and are especially common along streams and near the borders of woods, as well as in upland pastures and meadows.
"As the flight of these insects is weak, they have been obliged to resort to a number of tricks to outwit their enemies."
Read of these plans of escape in the article which begins on page 215 of Nature Library volume on BUTTERFLIES. A picture in full color appears facing page 225.

TREES TO BE WATCHED IN JULY

The Sorrel Tree

In late July or August it bears long branching racemes of tiny bell-shaped white flowers. Its vivid scarlet autumn foliage is its chief claim to the admiration of gardeners.
It is the sole representative of its genus in the world, so far as botanists know.
A description of the sorrel tree, its distribution, its growing habits, etc., will be found on page 122 of the Nature Library volume on TREES.

The American Linden or Basswood

The blossoms, cream-white and clustered on pale green leaf-like blades, open by hundreds in June and July, actually dripping with nectar, and illuminating the platforms of green leaves.
The flight of basswood seeds on the wing-like blades goes on through the winter.
On page 41 a picture of the basswood in full color is shown, and on page 70 will be found a description of this stately spreading tree.

The Mountain Laurel (See June)

NATURE'S PROGRAM

ANIMALS TO BE NOTED IN JULY

Grizzly Bear

The grizzlies mate in midsummer. Do you know how they challenge each other for the right to a hunting range?
The habits of grizzlies are described in an article beginning on page 232 of the Nature Library volume on ANIMALS, which is accompanied by a full-color illustration following page 234.

The Muskrat

In July the advance of winter is foreshadowed by the work of the muskrat in repairing an old home or in erecting a new one. Where shall we look to find him at this task? What does his home look like when finished?
In summer during the heat of the day muskrats may often be found swimming and floating about in the shadow of old willow trees. Description of these animals, their habits of mating, their food and shelter, etc., will be found in article beginning on page 116 of the Nature Library volume on ANIMALS.

AUGUST, The Maize Moon

If Rip Van Winkle awoke from his twenty-year slumber during August, he must have known at once what time of year it was, for this month has a look, a feel, even a sound, that is all its own.

Hay and grain fields have turned from green to yellow or tawny. Many are already harvested. The wild, uncultivated meadows are aglow with golden-rod, sprinkled with masses of the beautifully contrasted purple of the wild asters. Bird songs are no longer heard to any great extent. Instead, the air is full of the monotony of "insect music," the big cicada, or "harvest fly," winds up his buzzer and lets it run down repeatedly. "Dog-days-z-z-z-z-z-z-z" he seems to proclaim. In the fields a veritable "insect orchestra" fiddles and scrapes in the bright heat of the afternoon. Field crickets, katydids, long-horned grasshoppers; chwi-chwi-chwi—crrri-crri-crri—Katydid-katydid—retreat—retreat—retreat—treat.

And that is what the year seems to be doing—"retreating" before the slow but sure advance of winter. The floodtide of growth is past; Nature's whole thought now is of the future; she must make sure, in the warm weeks that remain, that all the multitude of lives, of plants, birds, insects, and animals, will be continued safely through the frosty time to another spring.

You can also learn the story of August from the feathery "ballooning" seeds of the dandelion, the milkweed, and the cat-tail. Blow on a puff-ball, as children do, and you see the little parachutes eddying away on the lightest breeze. They go to lodge in cultivated lawns, open meadows, anywhere and everywhere. The wind-carried seed is a wonderful invention of Mother Nature's; you will find it used by some of the most successful, widely distributed plants in the world, the thistle and milkweed, for instance.

The best, as well as the most interesting way to study Nature is to find out the reasons for things. Why, for instance, is the thistle prickly and hairy, even on the outsides of its very blossoms? Why does the milkweed exude its sticky fluid at the least scratch on stem or leaves? Let us try to answer these two questions and see how much more fascinating these plants become the moment we know their secret purposes.

The reason for the milkweed's "milk" has been explained by the naturalist Kerner.

Balloon Seeds of Dandelion

He noticed that the milky juice was especially abundant in the uppermost leaves and stems, and thought that it might be intended to prevent insects from crawling up into the blossoms for the honey. Since ants are particularly apt to climb plant stems for the nectar of the blossoms, Dr. Kerner started a number of ants to climbing a milkweed stalk. When they neared the summit, he noticed that at each movement of their feet, their sharp claws cut through the tender plant skin, and from the tiny wounds the milky juice began to flow, bedraggling the ants' feet and the hind parts of their bodies.

"The ants were much impeded in their movements," he writes, "and in order to rid themselves of the annoyance, drew their feet through their mouths. The movements, however, which accompanied these efforts simply resulted in making fresh scratches in the skin of the stem and fresh discharges of milky juice, so that the position of the ants became worse and worse. Many escaped by getting to the edge of a leaf and dropping to the ground. Others tried this method of escape too late, for the air soon hardened the milky juice into a tough brown substance, and after this happened all the strugglings of the ants to free themselves from the viscid matter were in vain."

Why does the milkweed thus punish the ants for attempting to get some of its nectar? Because these insects cannot be useful to the plant in securing a distribution of its fertilizing pollen to other milkweed plants. The Monarch Butterfly is the ideal carrier of pollen for the milkweeds, so they take this means of preserving their nectar for the Monarch alone.

The common "plumed thistle," whose pollen is carried from flower to flower by another butterfly, called the "Painted Lady," also jealously guards its nectar from the pilfering of ants. In this case, however, the intruders are kept away by the bristle-pointed hedge of hairy scales that surround the flower cup. One species also secures additional protection by a sticky strip around the cup just below the petals. This acts like "tangle-foot" fly-paper to any ants who are fortunate or unfortunate, enough to pass the prickly hedge.

The "Painted Lady"

When you have learned the true reasons for only a few of the wonderful structures seen in plants, birds, and insects, you will find yourself in a remarkable new world the existence of which you never suspected. In it flowers do not cease to be beautiful, but you see in them *more* than beauty. They become living individuals whose success, and very existence, depends upon the way in which they take advantage of the help of insects and winds in distributing their pollen and seeds. Butterflies are seen to be, not mere idle flutterers, but intently busy creatures with the welfare of their future offspring deeply at heart. They never live to see the children for which they are providing food by laying their eggs upon the proper food plant, but they give their whole brief lives to making sure of their future welfare.

And so a stroll in the fields of August, or any other month, may become, with a little accurate knowledge of Nature's methods, a remarkably broadening and uplifting experience, a sharpener of the eyes and the observation, and a guide to a finer appreciation of the wonderfully conceived universe we live in.

BIRDS MIGRATING SOUTHWARD IN AUGUST

Bobolink (See May)

Chat, Yellow-breasted (See May)

Flycatcher, Least Crested (See May)

Oriole, Orchard (See May)

Rail, or Sora Carolina (See May)

Sandpiper, Least (See May)

Warbler, Blackburnian (See May)

WILD FLOWERS APPEARING IN AUGUST

Arrow-head, Broad-leaved (See July)

Aster, Golden

Flowering Season: August and September.
Parts of Country Where Found: Long Island and Pennsylvania to the Gulf Coast.

AUGUST

Where to Look For: Dry soil or sandy; not far inland.
A description of this flower is to be found on page 235 of the Nature Library volume on WILD FLOWERS.

Aster, Large or Broad-leaved

Flowering Season: August and September.
Where to Look For: Dry, shady places.
See page 231 of the Nature Library volume on WILD FLOWERS for a description of this aster.

Aster, Low, Showy, or Seaside Purple

Flowering Season: August to November.
Parts of Country Where Found: Mostly near the coast from Massachusetts to Delaware.
Where to Look For: Dry, sandy soils.
This aster, one of the loveliest of all this beautiful clan, is described on page 234 of the Nature Library volume on WILD FLOWERS.

Aster, New England

Flowering Season: August to October.
Parts of Country Where Found: Canada, Massachusetts, and Minnesota to the Gulf.
Where to Look For: Swamps, moist fields, and roadsides.
A full-color illustration of the New England aster will be found facing page 225 of the Nature Library volume on WILD FLOWERS, while a description is given in article on page 233.

Aster, Late Purple

Flowering Season: August to October.
Parts of Country Where Found: Massachusetts and Minnesota to the Gulf.
Where to Look For: Dry, exposed places.
These solitary flowers, an inch across or more, are described on page 232 of Nature Library volume on WILD FLOWERS.

Aster, Dense-flowered, White-wreathed, or Starry

Flowering Season: August to November.
Parts of Country Where Found: Maine to Georgia and Texas, west to Arizona and British Columbia.
Where to Look For: Dry, open, sterile ground.
This aster, of which each minute flower-head measures only one

quarter inch across, is described on page 235 of the Nature Library volume on WILD FLOWERS.

Aster, White Wood

Flowering Season: August to October.
Parts of Country Where Found: Canada to Tennessee.
Where to Look For: Dry, open woodlands, thickets and roadsides.
See page 234 for description of this flower in Nature Library volume on WILD FLOWERS.

Beech-Drops

Flowering Season: August to October.
Parts of Country Where Found: New Brunswick west to Ontario and Missouri, south to the Gulf States.
Where to Look For: Under beeches, oaks, and chestnuts.
How is this pirate, with a disagreeable odor, branded a sinner by nature? And why? Read the article on Beech-drops on page 212 of the Nature Library volume on WILD FLOWERS for this and other interesting information.

Boneset (See July)

Brooklime (See April)

Bell-flower (See May)

Black-eyed Susan (See May)

Blue-eyed Grass (See May)

Butter-and-eggs; Yellow Toadflax

Flowering Season: June to October.
Parts of Country Where Found: Nebraska and Manitoba to Virginia and Nova Scotia; Europe and Asia.
Where to Look For: Waste lands, roadsides, banks, and fields.
This charming immigrant, meekly content with waste places, is rapidly inheriting the earth. For a description of its structure, habits, etc., see page 199 of Nature Library volume on WILD FLOWERS.

Camomile (See June)

Celandine (See April)

Chickweed (All Year)

Corn Cockle (See July)

Clover, Red (See April)

AUGUST

Dandelion, Common

Flowering Season: Every month in the year.
Parts of Country Where Found: Around the civilized world.
Where to Look For: Lawns, fields, grassy waste places.
"Fringing the dusty road with harmless gold," how has it managed without navies and armies to land its peaceful legions on every part of the civilized world and take possession of the soil? The structure, growing and seeding habits of this commonest and sunniest of flowers is described on page 254 of the Nature Library volume on WILD FLOWERS, and a full-color illustration to be found facing page 256.

Elecampane (See July)
Everlasting (See July)
Foxglove (See July)
Daisy, Common (See May)
Five Finger (See April)

Gentian, Closed, Bottle, or Blind

Flowering Season: August to October, according to place.
Parts of Country Where Found: Quebec to Manitoba and southward.
Where to Look For: Has a preference for moist soil.
This flower, of deep, intense blue, offers the bumblebee the last feast of the season. See page 168 of Nature Library volume on WILD FLOWERS where its structure, appearance, and habits are described.

Gerardia, Large Purple

Flowering Season: August to October.
Parts of Country Where Found: Northern U. S. to Florida, chiefly along the Atlantic Coast.
Where to Look For: Low fields and meadows; moist, sandy soil.
The fair face of gerardia gives no hint of the petty thefts done under cover of darkness in the soil below. What does it steal? Structure, habits, etc., are described on page 209 of Nature Library volume on WILD FLOWERS.

Gold Thread (See May)

Golden-rod, Blue-stemmed, Wreath, or Woodland

Flowering Season: August to October.
Parts of Country Where Found: Maine, Ontario, and Minnesota to the Gulf States.

Where to Look For: Shady roadsides; moist woods and thickets. Among golden-rods, none is prettier and more dainty than this common species. Described on page 227 of Nature Library volume on WILD FLOWERS.

Ground Nut (See July)

Hardhack (See July)

Golden-rod, Canada

Flowering Season: August to November.
Parts of Country Where Found: Arizona and Florida to British Columbia and New Brunswick.
Where to Look For: Dry soil.
This golden-rod is commonest of all the lovely clan east of the Rockies, and is pictured in full color on page 224 of the Nature Library volume on WILD FLOWERS. A descriptive section is to be found on page 229.

(For all other **Golden-rods**, see July)

Herb Robert (See May)

Joe-Pye Weed, Purple Thoroughwort

Flowering Season: August and September.
Parts of Country Where Found: New Brunswick to the Gulf, west to Manitoba and Texas.
Where to Look For: Moist soil, meadows, woods, and low ground.
Who was Joe Pye? And why did this flower receive his name? This purple thoroughwort, pictured in full color opposite page 209, is described, its structure and history given, on page 223 of Nature Library volume on WILD FLOWERS.

Mallow, Swamp Rose

Flowering Season: August and September.
Parts of Country Where Found: Massachusetts to the Gulf, west to Louisiana; found locally in the interior, but chiefly along the Atlantic seaboard.
Where to Look For: Brackish marshes, riversides, lake shores, saline situations.
Stately ranks of these magnificent flowers make the traveller exclaim at their amazing loveliness. See page 127 of Nature Library volume on WILD FLOWERS for description, appearance, structure, growth habits, etc.

AUGUST

Milkweed, Purple

Flowering Season: Summer.
Parts of Country Where Found: Eastern Massachusetts and Virginia to the Mississippi.
Where to Look For: Dry fields, woods, thickets.
Visited by humming-birds, butterflies, and other insects to which it is adapted to play host. See page 175 of Nature Library volume on WILD FLOWERS for means of identification.

Mustard, Field (See May)

Mustard, Hedge (See May)

Nightshade (See May)

Orchis, White-fringed (See July)

Orchis, Yellow-fringed (See July)

Peanut, Wild or Hog

Flowering Season: August and September.
Parts of Country Where Found: New Brunswick and Nebraska to the Gulf of Mexico.
Where to Look For: Moist thickets, shady roadsides.
Why should the same plant bear, as this does, two kinds of blossoms and leaves? And what is the poor excuse for branding this charming plant with a repellent folk-name? An account of the appearance, color, structure, habits, and uses of the wild peanut will be found on page 113 of Nature Library volume on WILD FLOWERS.

Pimpernel, Scarlet (See May)

Pokeweed (See June)

Primrose, Evening (See June)

Pickerel Weed(See June)

Pine Sap (See June)

Pipsissewa (See June)

Rose, Cherokee

Flowering Season: Summer.
Parts of the Country Where Found: Runs wild in the south.
Where to Look For: Thickets and roadsides.
"Climbing, rambling and rioting with a truly Oriental abandor

and luxuriousness" in its restricted belt, this flower may be identified through the description to be found on page 103 of Nature Library volume on WILD FLOWERS.

Rose, Swamp (See May)

Rattlesnake Weed (See May)

Raspberry, Purple Flowering (See June)

Sneezeweed; Swamp Sunflower

Flowering Season: August to October.
Parts of Country Where Found: Quebec and Northwest Territory to Florida and Arizona.
Where to Look For: Swamps, wet ground, banks of streams.
Many a pail of milk has been spoiled by a mouthful of this weed among the herbage.
Structure, appearance, manner of growth, etc., will be found described on page 243 of the Nature Library volume on WILD FLOWERS.

Self-heal (See May)

Speedwell (See May)

Skullcap (See May)

Star-grass (See May)

St. John's-wort (See June)

Sunflower, Tall or Giant

Flowering Season: August to October.
Parts of Country Where Found: Maine to Nebraska and Northwest Territory, south to the Gulf.
Where to Look For: Low ground, wet meadows, swamps.
The Indians put this plant to valuable uses—its stalk furnished them a textile fibre, its leaves fodder, its flowers a yellow dye, and its seeds, most valuable of all, food and hair oil! No wonder the early settlers prized it!
See page 242 for a description of its structure and habits, and the full-color illustration facing page 229 for its color and appearance in natural surroundings.

Toadflax (See May)

Vervain (See June)

Vetch (See June)

AUGUST

BUTTERFLIES TO BE WATCHED FOR IN AUGUST

The Diana Fritillary

Found only in a comparatively narrow range extending from West Virginia to Missouri, northward to Ohio and Indiana, and southward to Georgia and Arkansas.

The butterflies appear from the chrysalids from midsummer onward, and lay their eggs on or near violets in August or September. In this magnificent species the males are so unlike the females that only a skilled naturalist would even guess that they are related.

Perhaps if you know where there is iron-weed to watch, you may have the rare experience of capturing this lovely specimen. See page 118 for a description of this Fritillary, and page 129 for the full-color illustration in which the remarkable difference between the male and female is apparent.

The Parnassian Butterfly

To be found in Alaska and the higher elevations of the Rocky Mountains during the month of August.

Where ice forms at night and snow frequently falls by day these butterflies develop apparently in greater numbers than almost any of our other species are known to do in warmer regions.

Find how their structure and habits are adapted to the regions in which they make their habitat. Description is given on page 56 of the Nature Library volume on BUTTERFLIES.

The Black-bordered Yellow

Spread out over most of our Southern States, where it is abundant and widely distributed.

This tropical butterfly with its curious-looking chrysalis is described on page 105 of Nature Library volume on BUTTERFLIES.

SEPTEMBER, The Hunting Moon

"Labor Day" marks the end of vacation time for human beings, and is the signal for a return to more strenuous activity. But for Nature, September is the beginning of her resting period.

The first indication you may notice will be, perhaps, a prematurely yellowing tree in the woods, a forerunner of the gorgeous tapestry that will be spread on the trees next month.

What happens when a tree turns yellow or red in autumn? It is the outward indication of a wonderful process that is taking place in the leaves—the withdrawal from them, into the tree itself, of a remarkable substance called "cambium." The tree cannot afford to lose this precious material, and withdraws it from the leaves before they fall. Next month, the moon of the falling leaf, we will see how the trees manage to do this.

While you are strolling along the woodpaths this month you may notice here and there, in bushes and shrubs, what looks like a dead leaf, hanging or curled up, close to a twig. Every one is worth investigating, for it may prove to be something far more interesting than a withered leaf—namely, a cocoon. You ought to go "cocooning" this fall, this month or next. This kind of "hunting" will sharpen your powers of observation wonderfully, and store up for you a new kind of pleasure to enjoy next spring.

Bring home the cocoons you find, put them away in a shoe box and keep them, after identifying as many of the different kinds as you can, with the aid of the pictures of cocoons in the Nature Library volume on Butterflies. Lay each one on a piece of paper, marked with the name you have given it. Then, sometime next April, begin looking at your collection from time to time. During May you should be rewarded by seeing most of the butterflies and moths come out in all their beauty. You can then have the satisfaction of comparing each mature insect with its color picture in the Butterfly volume and finding out how accurate your identification of the cocoon was.

But September is not entirely occupied with preparing to tuck Nature's creatures in for their winter sleep. This month still has time and inclination for bringing out a few new flowers. "Better late than never" is September's motto in producing the beautiful, deep-blue "Fringed Gentian." It appears in this month, growing in low, moist meadows and woods, and continues blooming even into November's chilly days. Of it the poet Bryant wrote,

Cocoon on Leaf

> "Thou waitest late, and com'st alone
> When woods are bare and birds have flown,
> And frost and shortening days portend
> The aged year is near his end.
>
> "Then doth thy sweet and quiet eye
> Look through its fringes to the sky,
> Blue—blue—as if that sky let fall
> A flower from its cerulean wall."

But the woods and fields are not yet bare in September. In fact, they seem bent upon making a final burst of colorful beauty before settling down to neutral tints of gray and brown. The golden-rods and purple asters, a real harmony of contrasting colors, make the wild fields and tangled fence corners glow with loveliness; the sumachs are beginning to display their brilliant brick-red spikes. Shrubs show red berries where blossoms were in May and June. There is much of summer's opulence still left, and hints of autumn's coming grandeur. September is a month of transition from one kind of beauty to another.

Getting Ready to Migrate

And if you are particularly interested in our feathered friends, you will see evidences of a time of transition among them, too. All through birddom September sees a stirring, a preparation for some great coming event.

You will see the wild birds begin to flock on the telegraph wires, and among the weeds and shrubs along the streams. You will see the swallows, blackbirds, robins, and bluebirds, as they get together for their long southern flight.

"There are days in late September," writes Mr. Dallas Lore Sharp, "when the very air seems to be half of birds, especially toward nightfall, if the sun sets full and clear: birds going over; birds diving and darting about you; birds along the rails and ridge-poles; birds in the grass under your feet; birds everywhere. You should be out among them where you can see them. And especially you should see without fail, this autumn and every autumn, the wedge of wild geese cleaving the dull gray sky in their thrilling journey down from the far-off frozen North."

Many people who read this book will feel the charm

of Nature, but they are city dwellers and will say, "I'd love to know birds, flowers, butterflies, and trees, but I have no place to go but the city park. It isn't wild enough to see much in. If I lived in the country, as Mr. Sharp does, that would make it worth while."

Do not decide too soon that your city park is barren of interest for the student of any of Nature's wonders. Give it a trial first. Keep on walking in it, in the morning, in the evening, even at night with a flashlight. At first glance you may not see much, but when you have walked in it a number of times, you will begin to notice things that escaped you at first. Soon, each succeeding walk will show you *particular* things.

And the park, or whatever place you walk in, will share its secret surprises with you all the sooner if you go each time *expecting* to see something in particular—always looking for some special nest, plant, cocoon, or butterfly. You may not find what you are looking for that day, but your eyes will be sharpened by your expectation and purpose, and you will be all the surer to see something else just as interesting.

This guide will tell you what to look for and your Nature Library books will tell you how to identify them. At first you will need them in order to find out what the things you see are, and how they live and multiply. This in itself is a keen pleasure, but later, when the deep meaning of Nature begins to come home to you, you will taste the joy in her companionship that only a nature lover can know.

BIRDS MIGRATING SOUTHWARD IN SEPTEMBER

Bobolink (See May)

Bunting, Indigo (See May)

Chat, Yellow-breasted (See May)

Chickadee (See May)

Coot (See May)
Flycatcher, Crested (See May)
Flycatcher, Least Crested (See May)
Grosbeak, Rose-breasted (See May)
Kingbird (See May)
Oriole, Baltimore (See May)
Oriole, Orchard (See May)
Pewee, Wood (See May)
Plover, Semi-palmated or Ring-necked (See May)
Rail, Carolina; or Sora (See May)
Sandpiper, Least (See May)
Vireo, Warbling (See May)
Warbler, Blackburnian (See May)
Warbler, Yellow (See May)
Wren, Marsh (See May)
Yellowthroat, Maryland (See May)

FLOWERS THAT APPEAR IN SEPTEMBER

Arrow-head, Broad-leaved (See July)

Aster, Common Blue, Branching, Wood, or Heart-leaved

Flowering Season: September and October, even to December.
Parts of Country Where Found: New Brunswick to Minnesota and southward.
Where to Look For: Woods and shady roadsides.
Their mist-like masses hang from one to five feet above the earth. See page 231 of Nature Library volume on WILD FLOWERS.

Aster, Smooth or Blue

Flowering Season: September and October.
Parts of Country Where Found: Maine to Minnesota and southward.
Where to Look For: Dry soil and open woods.
Described for identification on page 234 of the Nature Library volume on WILD FLOWERS.

SEPTEMBER

Aster, White Heath

Flowering Season: September, even to December.
Parts of Country Where Found: Maine to Minnesota and southward.
Where to Look For: Dry soil.
This flower, one of whose names is "Farewell Summer," appears as a feathery mass of pink-tinged bloom till late in the fall. See page 235 of Nature Library volume on WILD FLOWERS for identification.

Bell Flower (See May)

Beech-drops (See August)

Black-eyed Susan (See May)

Buttercup, Common Meadow (See May)

Boneset (See July)

Brooklime (See April)

Camomile (See June)

Carrot, Wild (See June)

Celandine (See April)

Chickweed (See May)

Clover, Red (See April)

Clover, White (See May)

Corn Cockle (See July)

Daisy, Common (See May)

Dodder (See July)

Elecampane (See July)

Everlasting (See July)

Fleabane (See May)

Gentian, Fringed

Flowering Season: September to November.
Parts of Country Where Found: Quebec and Georgia westward beyond the Mississippi.

Where to Look For: Low, moist meadows and woods.
Because this flower is so rarely beautiful that few can resist the temptation of plucking it, it is becoming sadly rare near large settlements. Elusive as it is lovely, it seldom reappears in the same place year after year. Why is this so?
The structure and seeding habits of the fringed gentian are described in an article on page 167 of the Nature Library volume on WILD FLOWERS and a full-color illustration, giving an idea of its heavenly loveliness, faces page 128.

Gerardia, Large Purple, (See August)

Golden-rods (See July)

Ground Nut (See July)

Hard Hack (See July)

Herb Robert (See May)

Iron-weed (See July)

Jewel-weed (See July)

Jye Poe Weed (See August)

Ladies' Tresses (See July)

Lobelia, Great July (See July)

Lobelia, Red (See July)

Mallow, Rose (See August)

Meadow Rue, Tall (See July)

Mustard, Field (See May)

Mustard, Hedge (See May)

Milkweed, Purple (See August)

Nightshade (See May)

Parsnip, Wild (See June)

Pickerel Weed (See June)

Pine Sap (See June)

Pokeweed (See June)

Pond Lily, Yellow (See April)

SEPTEMBER

Primrose, Evening (See June)
Rattlesnake-weed (See May)
Self-heal (See May)
Star Grass (See May)
St. John's-wort (See June)
Toadflax (See May)
Vervain (See June)
Wintergreen, Creeping (See June)
Willow Herb, Great (See June)
Yarrow (See June)

Witch-hazel

Flowering Season: Autumn.
Where to Look For: Woods.
The yellow threadlike blossoms of this shrub are the last to appear in the autumn woods. See page 93 of the Nature Library volume on WILD FLOWERS for means of identification.

ANIMALS TO BE NOTED IN SEPTEMBER

Little Brown Bat

In late August and early September these graceful flyers are often seen in unusual numbers rushing about and chasing each other to and fro.
This common species of the Mammoth Cave of Kentucky (caves are preferred locations) is described in a fascinating article which begins on page 266 of the Nature Library volume on ANIMALS with a full-color illustration facing page 270.

OCTOBER, The Leaf-Falling Moon

From the first of October until its end, the eyes of the stroller in the woods and fields are filled with the beauty of the carnival of color with which the trees are bidding farewell to summer. We all admire the yellow, scarlet, and purple hues of the autumn leaves, but how many understand what causes them? Why do so many trees shed their leaves at the end of the growing season? Let us try to find out.

Even as early as July a tree (a horse-chestnut, for example) is beginning to prepare for the loss of its leaves in winter. Its winter buds, each containing the germ of a next year's leaf-shoot, are already formed by midsummer. And around the base of each mature leafstalk a well-marked line appears, indicating where the break will occur. Then a layer of corky cells forms on each side of this line, replacing the tough, fibrous tissue which, in the spring growing season, can be torn apart only by force. But now the corky cells at the joint weaken the hold of the leaf stem upon its twig, and when the moment of separation comes the lightest breath of wind—even the weight of the ripened leaf—will break it off.

But before this happens some very important work needs to be done by the tree, for the green leaves of summer contain great quantities of a very valuable substance called "cambium," and this the horse-chestnut tree cannot afford to lose with its leaves. So the thrifty tree undertakes to withdraw this "cambium," or leafpulp, before the fall of the leaves.

Slowly the green pulp is drained from the edges of the

leaves and is drawn back into the twigs through the stems. As the green "cambium" goes, it leaves behind much of the mineral matter that came up from the soil in the sap. Iron compounds and other minerals are left in the form of the red, yellow, and purple dyes that give the ripening leaves their gorgeous hues.

Finally, when the precious leaf pulp is all withdrawn safely into the branches, the leaf can fall without loss. Indeed, its fall will benefit the tree, for the decaying of the fallen leaves will return to the soil the mineral compounds that the roots will need for growth in spring seasons to come.

So you see that frost has very little to do in causing the autumn color of its trees. It can only hasten the process, or perhaps cut it short by throwing down the leaves before the tree has had time to withdraw all of its leaf pulp.

No one need complain because of his poor opportunity for studying Nature, provided he has the trees of a park to watch throughout the year. A keen pair of eyes used upon a single horse-chestnut tree for a whole year will surprise and inform the observer. It will indeed be a year of miracle.

In late October the lingering wild flowers are one by one succumbing to the nightly frosts. But there is at least one wild flower which will remain even until bleak November.

The Witch-hazel's "Artillery"

It is the witch-hazel. It has waited until late to bloom, but now the underwood begins to be brightened with the yellow of its fringy petals. Be careful, though, how you go too close to admire the witch-hazel's blossoms, or you may be shot! You may be hit in the face, or in the eye, by the missiles that this bush is ready to let fly at this time of the year.

In October, the witch-hazel carries "loaded pistols." They are the ripe seed-pods of last year's flowers. Each pod contains two long black seeds of bony hardness. The ripe pod splits in the frost, exposing the seeds. Then, as the pod dries and contracts still more, it finally and suddenly expels both its bullets, with surprising force, if your face happens to be the target. The witch-hazel can throw its seeds even to a distance of forty feet!

Why does it do this? Obviously, the shooting pistol pod is a clever device, invented for the witch-hazel by Mother Nature, in order to secure a wider distribution of the shrub's seed.

This invention accomplishes its purpose so well that it is used by a number of other plants. Even the "modest violet" becomes a sharpshooter in October. Every sunny day, even into November, its tiny pods can be seen popping open into three-cornered stars and scattering their tiny "shot" broadcast in all directions. If you have cultivated sweet peas in your garden during the summer you can watch something similar happening when their dried pods spring open on the dead vines in the late autumn.

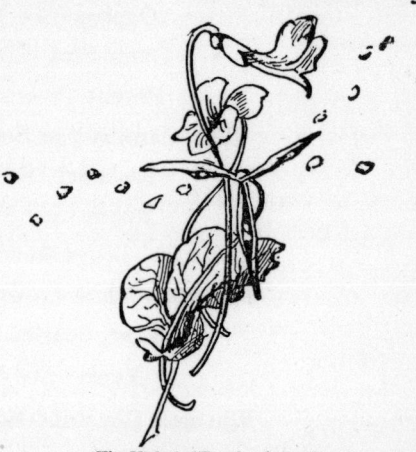

The Violet's "Bombardment"

Truly, every season has its wonders for the nature lover with a "seeing eye."

OCTOBER

BIRDS MIGRATING SOUTHWARD IN OCTOBER

Bittern (See May)
Blackbird, Red-winged (See March)
Bluebird (See March)
Bobolink (See May)
Coot (See May)
Goldfinch (See May)
Grackle, Bronzed (See March)
Hawk, Marsh (See March)
Hawk, Sparrow (See March)
Humming-bird, Ruby-throated (See May)
Osprey (See March)
Oven-Bird (See May)
Phœbe (See March)
Rail, Carolina; or Sora (See May)
Redstart (See May)
Robin (See March)
Shrike, Loggerhead (See May)
Sparrow, White-crowned (See May)
Tanager, Scarlet (See May)
Veery (See May)
Warbler, Chestnut-sided (See May)

WILD FLOWERS SEEN IN OCTOBER

Aster, Common Blue (See September)
Aster, Smooth or Blue (See September)
Aster, White Heath (See September)
Aster, Low, Showy, or Seaside Purple (See August)
Aster, New England (See August)

Aster, Late Purple (See August)
Aster, Dense-flowered (See August)
Aster, White Wood (See August)
Beech-drops (See August)
Camomile (See June)
Chickweed (See May)
Clover, Red (See April)
Clover, White (See May)
Daisy, Common (See May)
Fleabane (See May)
Gentian, Fringed (See September)
Gerardia, Large Purple (See August)
Golden-rod, Gray (See July)
Golden-rod, Wrinkle-leaved (See July)
Herb Robert (See May)
Jewel-weed (See July)
Ladies' Tresses (See July)
Lobelia, Great (See July)
Mustard, Field (See May)
Mustard, Hedge (See May)
Pokeweed (See June)
Primrose, Evening (See June)
Pickerel-weed (See June)
Pine Sap (See June)
Rattlesnake-weed (See May)
Self-heal (See May)
Star-grass (See May)
Toad-flax (See May)
Yarrow (See June)

OCTOBER

TREES TO BE WATCHED IN OCTOBER

Oak, the Scarlet

The scarlet oak is like a flaming torch set among the dull browns and yellows in our autumnal woods.
Features by which it may be identified are given in the description on page 59 of the Nature Library volume on TREES.

Oak, the Shingle or Laurel

In autumn the yellow, channelled midribs turn red, and all the blades to purplish crimson, and this color stays a long time.
This tree, its distribution and features of especial beauty are described on page 63 of the Nature Library volume on TREES.

Hornbeam, American

The paired nutlets are provided with a parachute each so that the wind can sow them broadcast. This wing is leafy in texture, shaped like a maple leaf, and curved into the shape of a boat.
Means for identifying this tree may be found on page 85 of the Nature Library volume on TREES.

Alder, the Seaside

This tree shares with the witch-hazel the peculiar distinction of bearing its flowers and ripening its fruit simultaneously in the fall of the year.
See page 92 of the Nature Library volume on TREES.

Gum, the Sour, or Black

In autumn patches of red appear as the leaves begin to drop. Soon the tree is a pillar of fire against yellowing ashes and hickories. No tree has a richer color than this one.
The range of this tree, the reason for its many names, means of identifying it, etc., will be found on page 96 of the Nature Library volume on TREES.

Gum, the Sweet

Wherever these gum trees grow, the autumn landscape is painted with the changeful splendor of the most gorgeous sunset. "The tree is not a flame, it is a conflagration!"
One recognizes the gum tree in winter by swinging seed-balls, an inch in diameter, like the balls of the buttonwood, except that those are smooth.

These seed-balls, the flowers, leaves, etc., of the sweet gum tree, are described on page 97 of the Nature Library volume on TREES. A full-color illustration appears on page 92.

The Witch hazel

Nowhere in summer would an undergrowth of witch-hazel trees attract attention. But in autumn, when other trees have reached a state of utter rest, the witch-hazel wakes and bursts into bloom.

Go into a witch-hazel thicket on some fine morning in early November and sit down on the drift of dead leaves that carpet the woods floor. The silence is broken now and then by a sharp report like a bullet striking against the bark of a nearby trunk, or skipping among the leaves. Where does the fusillade come from?

This very interesting tree is described on page 133 of the Nature Library volume on TREES, and a full-color illustration is shown on page 136.

Bush, the Burning

The burning bush lends its scarlet fruits to the vivid colors that paint any winter landscape. In October each is pale-purplish in color and a half inch across.

In Oklahoma and Arkansas and eastern Texas, the burning bush becomes a good-sized tree.

A description of this tree, in its various stages of growth, its uses, etc., will be found on page 136 of the Nature Library volume on TREES.

Sumach, the Staghorn

No tree carries its autumn foliage longer nor blazes with greater splendor in the soft sunshine of the late year. See page 138 for its identifying features, range, uses, etc., and page 138 for a full-color illustration.

Sumach, the Dwarf

In autumn the foliage mass changes to varying shades of scarlet and crimson. In the south the leaves are sometimes gathered in summer to be dried and pulverized for use in tanning leather.

The range and description of this tree are given in article on page 140 of the Nature Library volume on TREES.

Maple, the Sugar

In October the sugar maple paints the landscape with yellow and orange and red. This important and beautiful tree is described

OCTOBER

on page 194 of the Nature Library volume on TREES and on page 200 is illustrated in full color.

Ash, the Red

Very gradually an ash tree launches its seeds. It is easy to understand why the family is so scattered through any woods, for the wind is the sower of the long and slender seeds. Described on page 205 of the Nature Library volume on TREES.

Walnut, the Southwestern

In autumn the foliage turns bright yellow. See page 29 of the Nature Library volume on TREES.

ANIMALS TO BE WATCHED IN OCTOBER

Skunk

By the last of October after the lush autumn season the skunks roll and totter about on their weasel feet that seem much too small to support an animal of so much weight and dignity.

They mate from the first to the middle of March and the young are born about the end of April or early May. In February a skunk is hardly recognizable as the heavy-bodied sluggard of autumn.

On page 217 of the Nature Library volume on ANIMALS is given an account of the habits of the skunk, and on page 203 a full-color illustration will be found.

NOVEMBER, The Mad Moon

"The north wind doth blow,
And we shall have snow,
And what will the robin do then,
Poor thing?"

Most of us know very well what tne robin will do. In fact, he has done it already, and is even now getting fatter and saucier than ever, upon the worms and grubs of the sunny southland. So this removes him far from any need of our pity, along with all our other summer friends who have wings.

But most of us do not know what the woodland people who have no wings are going to do to escape the bitter cold of the months that are coming—the muskrat, the chipmunk, the woodchuck, the field mouse, the frog in the pond and ditch. They cannot migrate far away upon the highway of the air. They must stay. How do they keep from freezing and starving?

The north wind is sweeping the hard stubble fields and shaking the leafless branches. Woodchuck's fur coat is indeed warm, but his sweet clover hay and other foods are all gone. He cannot eat through all the coming winter. What does he do? His philosophy is simple. If he cannot eat, he will do the next best thing: he will sleep.

The Woodchuck and His Hole

So late fall finds Woodchuck all ready, with his winter food stored up within his own skin. He has eaten

NOVEMBER

until no more fat could be squeezed within his baggy hide. He is enormously corpulent. He has dug until his hole is down, down, five feet down, just below the level to which Jack Frost usually reaches with his freezing fingers. Here he will curl up and sleep; at least until "Ground Hog Day," and perhaps still later.

And what does Chipmunk do when the north wind comes, bringing the frost? He also has made his bed deep down under the stone fence, but he will not sleep all the time, for he has spent half the summer amassing a store of acorns and nuts—enough to set his frugal underground table until the first warm spring days.

And what does Muskrat do? In summer you saw his little beady eyes peeping out from the opening of his tunnel at the edge of the ditch in the marshy meadows. But the tunnel will not be a good place to spend the cold weather. The autumn floods will fill it and the frost will freeze the water solid. The simplest thing to do is to build a winter house upon a grassy tussock, above the water's reach. So Muskrat joins his labors to those of two or three of his neighbors and relatives. They all turn architects and masons and build the walls of the dome-like house with loads of mud-and-reed mortar. By the end of November they have finished a fine weather and cold-proof lodge. It has no doors above ground, but opens below into the water under the ice, and that means that food is in reach whenever needed—under the meadow ice the roots of the sedges are still succulent and tender—there is a choice of menu, too—calamus roots, iris, and arum. Surely Muskrat, in his cosy lodge, needs no more pity from us than Robin, far away in a warmer clime!

But surely the frog will perish. He has no skill as a builder of shelters or as a digger of deep holes. The best he can do is to wriggle into the mud at the bottom of the shallow pond. Surely Jack Frost will find him there and freeze him solid. "Let him!" says the philosophical spring peeper. And that is just what often happens, but without killing or even harming the frog. He will thaw out again, as good as new, in the spring. He passes the winter in a state of "suspended animation" rather than in sleep. Even his heart may freeze solid: he does not know or care.

But all the birds have not gone south in November, and many of them will not go at all. Chickadees, kinglets, juncos, partridges, goldfinches, and tree sparrows, blue jays, downy woodpeckers, hairy woodpeckers, flickers, nuthatches, snow buntings, purple finches, cedar waxwings, grosbeaks, shrikes, not to mention numerous members of the tribes of hawks and owls—all can be seen in the northern winter. Those of you who are bird-students need have no lack of occupation, even though the snow drifts deep along the fences.

Foraging for Weed Seeds

And if you are a bird-lover, you do not need to be told how much these cheerful companions of the snows will appreciate a few handfuls of grain, or a large lump of suet tied to a branch in your garden or in the city park, where they can find it easily.

And if you are expecting to have a garden, or are a farmer, you ought to give the winter birds food regularly simply as a thank-offering, a small return for the good service they perform for you every summer.

Here is the story of the benefits conferred upon man by only one bird, the chickadee. It is told by Mr. Forbush, ornithologist of the state of Massachusetts.

Some years ago Mr. Forbush set out to make his orchard particularly attractive to chickadees and other birds during the winter, with a view to finding out what they ate. Various kinds of food were offered them; but this did not prevent the birds from doing foraging on their own account. It was found that the eggs of the cankerworm and tent caterpillar, and of other enemies of trees, formed their principal diet. After studying the meals of the chickadees particularly, Mr. Forbush found that a single bird could eat over 250 cankerworm eggs at a meal. In a day it might destroy more than twice that number.

It was also ascertained that in late March and early April, when the cankerworm moths were hatching out and preparing to lay their eggs, each chickadee would devour over thirty of the moths every day. When you realize that each of these moths would have laid 180 eggs, you can put it down to the chickadee's credit that he prevented the birth of about 5,000 cankerworm eggs in one day.

And now for the proof. Mr. Forbush and his neighbor treated the birds as friends and partners, attracted them with food when they needed it, and their trees bore luxuriant foliage and produced a good crop of fruit; while elsewhere in the town, most of the apple trees were stripped of their leaves and very few produced any fruit that year.

"Year after year," Mr. Forbush wrote, "we have kept our trees free from serious insect injury, without spraying or otherwise protecting the foliage, merely by a little effort and expenditure to attract the birds and furnish them safe homes."

Winter is really the best season in which to begin the study of birds, because there are then fewer of them, and we are not discouraged by the overwhelming number of varieties demanding our attention, as is the case at migration time and in the summer.

NATURE'S PROGRAM
BIRDS MIGRATING SOUTHWARD IN NOVEMBER

Cowbird (See March)
Catbird (See May)
Dove, Mourning (See March)
Finch, Purple (See March)
Grackle, Purple (See March)
Killdeer (See March)
Kingfisher, Belted (See March)

WILD FLOWERS TO BE SEEN IN NOVEMBER

Aster, Common Blue (See September)
Aster, White Heath (See September)
Aster, Low, Showy, or Seaside (See August)
Aster, Dense-flowered, White-wreathed (See August)
Camomile (See June)
Chickweed (See May)
Clover, Red (See April)
Clover, White (See May)
Daisy, Common (See May)
Fleabane (See May)
Golden-rod, Gray (See July)
Golden-rod, Wrinkle-leaved (See July)
Mustard, Field (See May)
Mustard, Hedge (See May)
Yarrow (See June)

DECEMBER, The Long Night Moon

Over sixty years ago one of the greatest nature lovers who ever lived wrote in his diary:
"Another bright winter's day, to the woods to see what birds' nests are made of."

If we are tempted to feel that the December out of doors has little to repay us for the effort of going for a stroll in the woods, we shall do well to follow the example of Thoreau. Many winter walkers before and since his time have made an investigation of birds' nest materials one of their winter hobbies.

This leafless time furnishes a splendid opportunity, for dozens of nests which were completely concealed by the summer foliage are now entirely revealed to the gaze of the most careless searcher. And what a great variety of building materials you will find worked into them!

Until you have time to go out into the December groves and find an example for yourself, let us look at the make-up of the gray vireo's nest through the eyes of William Hamilton Gibson, who described it many years ago in his book, "Sharp Eyes."

He found that the stout strands which secured the nest in the fork of a maple branch were selected fibres of inner tree bark, spider and cocoon silk, and strips from the milkweed stalk.

"The compact body of the nest," Mr. Gibson wrote, "gives a singular variety; here are strips of white and yellow birch bark, aster calyxes, cobwebs, a blue-bottle fly, spider-egg silk tufts, slender roots, bits of pith, skeletonized leaves, pine-needles, old cocoons of the tussock-moth, grass, caterpillar hairs, dandelion seeds, moss, and feathers. A broad piece of mottled gray, paper-like substance forms the outside base of the nest. We might have been certain of finding this—a fragment of hornet's nest, one of the favorite fabrics of all the vireos. And what is this white weather-beaten fragment which crops out beneath it? A bit of newspaper!

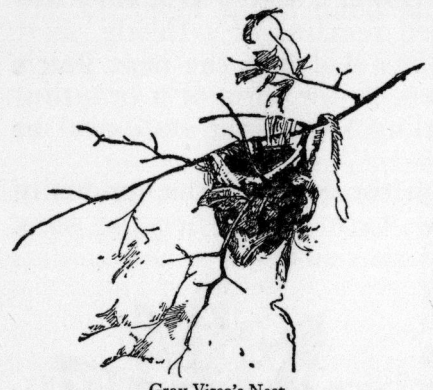

"But I have not begun to mention all the curious things that are woven into a vireo's fabric. I once found one which was decorated with a hundred or more black, shiny caterpillar skins. Another showed the gauzy mitten of a toad. Another a half-yard of lace edging. And only last year I discovered the most singular specimen of all—a real novelty even for a vireo—a nest almost entirely composed of *snake skins*."

Gray Vireo's Nest

It will be seen that even a single bird may have a very wide choice of nesting materials. Many species, however, have "specialties," for which they show special preferences. A few of these follow, selected from a list made by Mr. Gibson:

Wren	feathers
Chipping sparrow	horsehair and roots
Snowbunting	fox hair
Worm-eating warbler	hickory and chestnut catkins
Ovenbird	dried spore stems of mosses
Purple finch	hog bristles and horsehair
Robin	grass and mud
Baltimore oriole	milkweed bark, horsehair and long moss
Humming-bird	fern wool, red oak leaf down

Almost everyone knows that the "winter buds" upon the trees contain next year's green leaf shoots in miniature, and that they are formed the previous summer and held in readiness for the following spring's opening.

But perhaps not many people know that if they will follow downward the dried remains of a thistle, as it sticks out of the snow, they will find the next year's thistle plant, already green, in the form of a beautiful flat rosette of leaves, nestling around the stalk next to the ground.

Here it hides all through the cold months, gradually growing, and awaiting the warm days when the snow shall be gone, and the already formed leaves shall have their opportunity to shoot upward. Many a dried stalk, protruding above the snow, will guide you to the discovery of a green, fully formed plant at its base upon the ground. Moth-mullein, peppergrass, the evening primrose, the willow herb, or fireweed, and the rib plantain, all take this method of advance growth in flat form.

A Winter Rosette

One naturalist has given a very clear idea of these rosettes by imagining the fully grown plant, as we see it in summer, to consist of an elastic rubber band fully stretched. If this elastic stem were allowed to contract fully, the plant would look exactly as the winter rosette of the same plant does. Like the winter buds of trees, the winter rosettes of plants are a device of Nature's to get a "head start" of the spring season when it finally comes. They may be found, in some instances, as early as September, and remain green all winter.

BIRDS RESIDENT IN THE NORTH THROUGH THE WINTER

Gull, Herring

Parts of Country Where Found: Nests from Minnesota and New England north, especially about the St. Lawrence, Nova Scotia, Newfoundland, and Labrador. Winters from Bay of Fundy to West Indies and Lower California.
Times of Appearance: Winter resident. Migrates southward in March, north in November
For color of young and old, food habits, value as scavengers, etc., see article on page 244 of the Nature Library volume on BIRDS. For color, appearance, and identifying marks, see full-color illustration facing page 242.

Junco

Parts of Country Where Found: Breeds from the tree limit to the northern U. S. in mountains as far south as Pennsylvania; winters throughout the eastern U. S. and southern Ontario, south to the Gulf Coast; casual in California, Arizona, and New Mexico; straggles to Siberia.
Times of Appearance: Winter resident in the north. Migrates southward in September, northward in April.
For food habits, sociability, call note, as well as appearance and marks of identification, see page 104 of the Nature Library volume on BIRDS.

Loon

Parts of Country Where Found: Northern part of Northern Hemisphere. In North America breeds from northern U. S. to Arctic Circle and winters from northern U. S. to Gulf of Mexico.
Times of Appearance: A wandering winter resident in the north. Most common in the migrations from September to May, except in mountain lakes.
For identifying marks, calls, winter wanderings, remarkable diving and swimming habits, nesting habits, see article on page 247 of the Nature Library volume on BIRDS. A full-color illustration faces page 243.

Nuthatch, White-breasted

Parts of Country Where Found: British provinces to Mexico; eastern United States.
Times of Appearance: Common resident, most prominent in winter. Migrates southward in October, northward in April.

DECEMBER

For article giving color, appearance, and identifying marks, acrobatics, food and song, etc., see article on page 38 of the Nature Library volume on BIRDS.

Nuthatch, Red-breasted

Parts of Country Where Found: Breeds in Canada south to Minnesota, Michigan, and Massachusetts, farther in mountain ranges; winters from southern Canada to Lower California and the Gulf States.
Times of Appearance: Irregular winter resident. Migrates northward August and September or later; southward in April or May. On page 40 of the Nature Library volume on BIRDS is given description of this bird, its food habits, song, the origin of its name, etc. A full-color illustration faces page 46.

Shrike, Northern

Parts of Country Where Found: Breeds in North America above the U. S., south in winter to the middle U. S.
Times of Appearance: A roving winter resident. Migrates southward in November, north in April.
This bird is nicknamed the "butcher-bird." The reason for this, with a description of the shrike, its food habits, song, etc., is to be found in article on page 77 of the Nature Library volume on BIRDS.

Snowflake, or Snow Bunting

Parts of Country Where Found: Breeds in the Arctic zone; winters in Canada and northern U. S.
Times of Appearance: Winter visitor. Migrates southward in November; northward in March.
See article on page 105 of the Nature Library volume on BIRDS for means of identification, food habits, etc.

Sparrow, Field

Parts of Country Where Found: Breeds throughout eastern U. S., winters from Missouri and New Jersey (casually farther north) to the Gulf Coast.
Times of Appearance: A few are resident in winter in the north. Migrate northward in March and early April; southward in October.
For description, habitat, song, etc., see article on page 108 of the Nature Library volume on BIRDS.

Sparrow, Fox

Parts of Country Where Found: Breeds from the tree limit to Alberta and Newfoundland; winters chiefly south of Illinois and Virginia; occasional stragglers remain north most of the winter.
Times of Appearance: Migrates northward in March, southward in November. Most common in migrations.
For article on color, appearance, identifying marks, call and song, food habits, etc., see page 105 of the Nature Library volume on BIRDS.

Sparrow, Song

Parts of Country Where Found: Various races, varying in color from very pale (Desert Song Sparrow) to very dark (Sooty Song Sparrow) are found locally throughout North America, from the fur countries to the Southern States. Only one race is found throughout the East, breeding in the Northern States and wintering as far south as the Gulf Coast.
Times of Appearance: A few remain in the north all year. Migration is northward in March, southward in November.
For description, identifying marks, song, etc., see page 106 of the Nature Library volume on BIRDS.

Sparrow, Swamp

Parts of the Country Where Found: North America east of the plains, breeding in Canada and the Northern States. Winters from Nebraska and Massachusetts to the Gulf Coast.
Times of Appearance: A few winter in the north. Migration is northward in April and early May; southward in October.
An article describing the swamp sparrow, with its identifying marks, habitat, nest, song, etc., is to be found on page 108 of the Nature Library volume on BIRDS.

Sparrow, Tree

Parts of Country Where Found: Breeds in Canada; winters in southern Canada and the Northern States.
Times of Appearance: Winter resident in north. Migrates southward in October and November; northward in April.
Color, appearance, markings, food habits, song, etc., are all described on page 110 of the Nature Library volume on BIRDS.

DECEMBER

Waxwing, Cedar

Parts of Country Where Found: North America, from northern British provinces to Kansas and North Carolina; winters throughout the U. S. and down to Central America.
Times of Appearance: A roving resident, without fixed migration seasons.
For appearance, color, markings of identification, see full-color illustration facing page 71, and for description of habits, food, nest, call-notes, etc., see article on page 80 of the Nature Library volume on BIRDS.

JANUARY, The Snow Moon

We have seen how the provident chipmunk, imitating the bee's industry, lays up a store of nuts and acorns, and spends the winter far underground. The red squirrel is also a hoarder of winter food—but the big gray squirrel will have nothing of their foresight. Sufficient unto the day is the hunger thereof. That is his motto. He is a true winter "tramp," picking up a handout wherever he may find it.

So we see him abroad all winter, scampering over the snow, frisking up tree trunks, and peeping around them at us as we take our winter walk in the woods. But he is not abroad merely for exercise. Exercise like his develops an appetite in frosty air; you may depend upon it he is looking for a dinner.

Watch him a little while and see how he gets it. Now he is bounding over the light snow crust, but now he pauses, sniffs repeatedly, and suddenly begins to burrow in the snow. Now he is lost to sight, but if the snow is not too deep, we may still follow his progress by the cracking and quaking of the surface above the tunnel he is making. A little farther on he suddenly reappears, a small pine cone in his teeth. Away he goes to bite off the scales, and devour the seeds.

Gray Squirrel Finds a Dinner

If we approach the spot where he obtained the pine cone under the snow, we shall probably find the surface

JANUARY

crust cracked and heaved up in various directions for several feet. These surface breaks indicate the lines of a system of tunnels which our gray forager has made under the snow in his search for cones and other edibles with which to break his fast.

You have all heard of "the January thaw." Sometimes it fails to come at all, but if it does, there are a few days when the icicles drip and fall from the eaves, and spring seems just around the corner.

If this mild period comes you may be astonished to see a large butterfly fluttering about in the woods.

It has dark wings with a yellow edge and its true name is *Vanessa antiopa*. The specimens you sometimes see on mild days in winter were hatched out late in the fall, and spent the cold weather hiding beneath loose

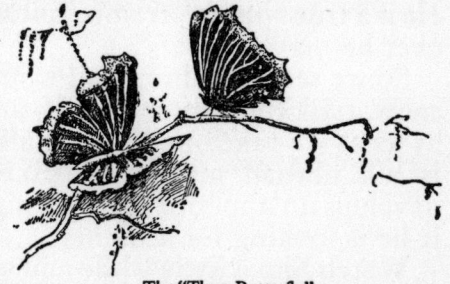

The "Thaw Butterfly"

clapboards in barns, under loose shingles of roofs, or in the edges of abandoned hay stacks in the field. They have also been found wintering under the loosened bark of old stumps. But the moment the sun warms the air and the snow melts a little, out they come for an airing.

If you know where a white birch tree grows, do not neglect walking under it on your January walk, particularly if it has snowed within a day or two, for under it you will find the whitened ground peppered with curious little specks. Under your magnifying glass each one will look like a miniature eagle or hawk, with wings and tail spread.

The Birch's Seed Catkins

What are they? Throw a club up into the branches above, and your question will be answered by a shower of more of the tiny "seed-birds" from the birch's seed catkins. If you can reach and secure one of these seed-holders whole, you can perform a pretty experiment by pinching off the hard little scale at the tip. This frees the whole mass of seeds, and they will fall in a steady cascade, until only a bare stem is left. Since each catkin contains nearly a thousand of the "birds," it is no wonder that you sometimes see whole groves of closely set white birches.

January, like December, is also a good month to begin studying birds. There are over sixty kinds to be seen in the northeastern parts of our country. These are either "permanent residents," or "winter visitors." The latter are birds which spend their summers far in northern Canada or the Arctic, and their winters in our comparatively milder climate.

TREES TO WATCH IN JANUARY
American Elm; White Elm

Winter offers the best opportunity for the study of tree forms. Our common elm shows at least five different patterns: vase form, plume form, oak tree form, weeping willow form and feathered elm. Growing everywhere east of the Rocky Mountains, not to know this tree is a mark of indifference. It is hardy and cheerful, reflecting the indomitable spirit of the pioneer, whom it accompanied from the Eastern States into the treeless territories of the Middle West.

This tree, with its spring loveliness, its summer luxuriance, its flowers, seeds, etc., is described on page 210 of the Nature Library volume on TREES, and a full-color illustration is shown opposite page 216.

The Red Maple

In winter, the lover of the woods, revisiting the scenes of his summer rambles, knows the scarlet maple by the knotty, full-budded twigs which gleam like red-hot needles set with coral beads.

JANUARY

It is described in an article on page 195 of the Nature Library volume on TREES.

The Post Oak

In winter the post oak keeps its cloak of harsh-feeling, thick, coarse-veined leaves. Other features by which it may be identified are described on page 52 of the Nature Library volume on TREES.

The Black Walnut

Hidden in the ground, the shell absorbs moisture and winter frost cracks it by gentle but irresistible force. So the plantlet has no hindrance to its growth when spring comes. The succeeding stages of its growth to a majestic tree, with luxuriant crown, are described in article beginning on page 31 of the Nature Library volume on TREES, and a full-color illustration opposite page 8 gives an idea of its appearance.

ANIMALS TO WATCH IN JANUARY

Canadian Beaver

All winter these restless animals move about under the ice searching out roots and gnawing into bushes.
Their habits in other seasons, their burrows, their remarkable building ability, their methods of communicating with each other, their enemies, with many other interesting details of these most interesting creatures, are described in an article beginning page 96 of the Nature Library volume on ANIMALS. A full-color illustration is shown opposite page 110.

Woodland Caribou; American Reindeer

Gregarious animals have usually many means of communication with their fellows. With the caribou, the sudden elevation of the white tail, when danger is sensed, is a silent alarm immediately understood by the nearest of their kind.
The hoof of the caribou is one of the most wonderful of Nature's adaptations to special necessities to environment. In the season of deep snows the frog is entirely absorbed and the edges of the hoof, now quite concave, grow out in thin, sharp ridges.
A fascinating account of this animal, its habits and character, etc., is to be found on page 31 of the Nature Library volume on ANIMALS, with a full-color illustration facing page 30.

Red Squirrel

Where red squirrels abide tunnels are often found driven here and there through the snow, always quite near the ground.
A description of these sociable animals, their preferred environment, their nests, young, food, and seasonal habits is to be found beginning page 64 of the Nature Library volume on ANIMALS, and a full-color illustration faces page 67.

Snowshoe Rabbit

This little animal, in winter a pure white with tinges of brown below the surface, would be unrecognizable if met in summer with its dress of very different hues. This variation, which puzzled early naturalists, is not due to an actual change in color but to a moult.
The extremely interesting characteristics and habits of these hares are discussed in an article beginning on page 135 of the Nature Library volume on ANIMALS.

Prairie Hare

The prairie hare is a solitary, seldom associating with its fellows except at time of mating. Its distribution, home, food, enemies, etc., are noted in an account given on page 141 of the Nature Library volume on ANIMALS.

FEBRUARY, The Hunger Moon

The person who is just beginning to be a "nature-hiker" through the woods and fields will soon be struck by the small number of four-footed creatures he meets, as compared with the abundance of other objects of interest. He sees the birds and butterflies flying about, or poised quite near on bush or tree. The trees and flowers are, of course, stationary and easily observed and examined. But if he catches a glimpse of a fox, or a rabbit, or a woodchuck, or a deer, it is usually at quite a long distance, and for a few seconds only. And, in fact, these meetings with animals are usually rare events, especially near towns.

This is true because, for one thing, most of the four-footed folk are nocturnal in their habits, hiding quietly by day. We cannot tell what they do by night, for the fields and woodlands where their activities take place tell no tales.

But wait! There is one exception; one time when every meadow and clearing in the woods keeps an exact record of its nightly events, and writes them plainly for every eye that understands the language. This happens when it snows.

If you believe that animal life is scarce in your neighborhood, go out early some morning in February after there has been a light fall of snow during the night. You will probably be amazed! If you like a good story, you will do well to follow up all the tracks you see in the snow, for they tell some that are indeed both interesting and thrilling. And if you like detective stories, you can have the opportunity to do some real "sleuthing" on your own account. Here is a very simple problem to solve as a starter.

These are the prints of the four feet of a galloping hare, or little gray rabbit. Can you tell, just by looking at these footprints, which pair were made by the front feet, and which pair by the hind ones? Don't guess. Try to imagine the way the rabbit gallops; or try to imagine how *you* would gallop if you went on four feet, and then decide. And be careful; most people get it wrong. When you can solve a simple problem like this in detective work, you will be ready to go on and reconstruct, entirely from close observation, such a tragedy in the snow as this one, observed and described by Mr. Ernest Thompson Seton. But please note that he did not actually see any of these things happen. He reconstructed the whole occurrence from the "evidence," exactly as a good detective does at the scene of a crime.

The Rabbit's "Autograph"

The Fox's Story in the Snow

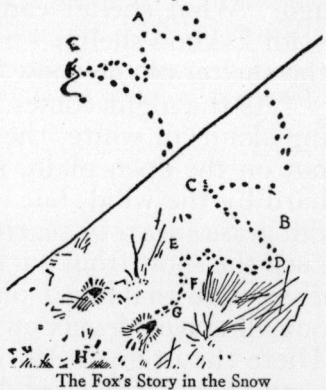

"For a mile or two I followed my fox. Nothing happened. I got only the thought that his life was largely made up of nose investigation and unfavorable reports from the committee in charge. Then we came to a long, sloping hollow. The fox trotted down this, and near its lower end he got a nose report of importance, for he had swung to the right and gone slowly—so said the short steps—zigzagging up the wind. Within fifteen feet, the tracks in the course shortened from four or five feet to nothing, and ended in a small hole in a bank. From this the fox had pulled out a common harmless garter snake, torpid, curled up there doubtless to sleep away the winter. The fox chopped the snake across the spine with his powerful meat-cutters, killed it thus, dropped it on the snow, and then, without eating a morsel of it as far as I could see, he went on with his hunt. (See illustration at A.)

"The dotted guide led me now, with many halts and devious turns, across a great marsh. On the far end the country was open in places, with clumps of timber, and into this, from the open marsh, had blown a great bank of soft and drifted snow.

"The blizzard is a terror to wild life out on the plains. When it comes the biggest, strongest, best clad, rush for shelter. They know that to face it means death. The prairie chickens or grouse have learned the lesson long ago. What shelter can they seek? There is only one —an Eskimo shelter—a snow house. They can hide in the shelter of the snow.

"As the night comes, with the fearful frost and driving clouds of white, the chickens dive into a snowdrift; not on the open plain, for there the snow is hammered hard by the wind, but on the edge of the woods, where tall grass spears or scattering twigs stick up through and keep the snow from packing. Deep in this the chickens dive, each making a place for itself. The wind wipes out all traces, levels off each hole and hides them well. There they remain till morning, warm and safe, unless —and here is the chief danger—some wild animal comes by during the night, finds them in there, and seizes them before they can escape.

"This chapter of grouse history was an old story to the fox and coming near the woodland edge, his shortened steps showed that he knew it for a Land of Promise. (See illustration at B.)

"At C he came to a sudden stop. Some wireless message on the wind had warned him of game at hand. He paused here with foot upraised. I knew it, for there was his record of the act. The little mark there was not a track, but the paw-tips' mark, showing that the fox had not set the foot down, but held it poised in a pointer dog pose, as his nose was harkening to the tell-tale wind.

"Then from C to D he went slowly, because the steps were so short, and now he paused: the promising scent was lost. He stood in doubt, so said the tell-tale snow in the only universal tongue. Then the hunter turned and slowly worked toward E, while frequent broad touches in the snow continued the guarantee that the maker of these tracks was neither docked nor spindle-tailed.

"From E to F, the shortened steps, with frequent marks of pause and pose, showed how the scent was warming—how well the fox knew some good thing was near.

"At F he stood still for some time with both feet set down in the snow, so it was written. Now was the critical time, and straight up the redolent wind he went, following his nose, cautiously and silently as possible, realizing that now a single heedless step might spoil the hunt.

"At G were the deeply imprinted marks of both hind feet, showing where the fox sprang just at the moment when, from the spotless snowdrift just ahead, there broke out two grouse that had been slumbering below. Away they went with a whirr, whirr, fast as wing could bear them; but one was just a foot too slow; the springing fox secured him in the air. At H he landed with him on the prairie, and had a meal that is a fox's ideal in time of plenty; and now, in deep hard winter, it must have been a banquet of delight.

FEBRUARY

"Now for the first time I saw the meaning of the dead garter snake far back on the trail. Snake at no time is nice eating, and cold snake on a cold day must be a mighty cold meal. Clearly the fox thought so. He would rather take a chance of getting something better. He killed the snake, so it could not get away. It was not likely any one would steal from him that unfragrant carcass, so he would come back and get it later if he must.

"But as we see, he did not have to do so. His faith and patience were amply justified. Instead of a cold, unpleasant snake, he fed on a fine hot bird.

"Thus I got a long, autobiographical chapter of fox life by simply following his tracks through the snow. I never once saw the fox himself that made it, and yet I know—and you know—it to be true as I have told it."

And so you see that the nature student does not always have to see a fox or any other animal with his eyes in order to know it is there, and to know how it lives and acts. Surely spending leisure time in the open is well worth while, if it confers powers of observation such as those evidenced by Mr. Seton in reading this "snow-story" of the fox's hunting.

TREES TO BE WATCHED IN FEBRUARY
The Pussy Willow

A walk in the woods in late February often brings us this charming surprise of a meeting with this little tree just when its gray pussies are pushing out from their brown scales. In midsummer the pussy willow is lost among the shrubby growth in any woods. See description on page 84 of the Nature Library volume on TREES.

ANIMALS TO BE WATCHED IN FEBRUARY
Woodchuck

Popular superstition of unknown origin has it that the woodchuck arises from his winter torpor on February 2nd.

He becomes by October fat, to an almost ridiculous state of obesity.

His many characteristic habits, his food preferences, his burrow, his mating, etc., are all described in an article beginning on page 89 of the Nature Library volume on ANIMALS. A full-color illustration of the woodchuck in his natural surroundings appears opposite page 95.

BIRDS WHICH RESIDE PERMANENTLY THROUGHOUT THEIR RANGE

Bob-White, or Quail

Parts of Country Where Found: Eastern U. S. and southern Ontario, from southern Maine to the South Atlantic and Gulf States; west to central South Dakota and eastern Texas, and spreading in the West.
Permanent Resident Throughout Range.
For description, means of identification, food preferences, nest, habits, etc., etc., see page 206 of the Nature Library volume on BIRDS. For color markings, and appearance in natural surroundings, see full-color illustration facing page 211.

Buzzard, or Turkey Vulture

Parts of Country Where Found: Temperate North America, from coast to coast, rarely so far north as British Columbia, southward to Patagonia and Falkland Islands. Casual in New England.
Permanent Resident, except at northern limit of range.
For description, means of identification, food preferences, nest, habits, etc., etc., see page 196 of the Nature Library volume on BIRDS.

Cardinal

Parts of Country Where Found: Eastern U. S. A southern bird, becoming more and more common in the summer in states north of Virginia, especially in Ohio, south of which it is resident throughout the year.
Resident rather than migrating birds, usually remaining in localities to which they have found their way.
For description, means of identification, food preferences, nest, habits, etc., etc., see page 101 of the Nature Library volume on BIRDS. For color markings, and appearance in natural surroundings, see full-color illustration facing page 98.

FEBRUARY

Crow

Parts of Country Where Found: Throughout North America, from Hudson Bay to the Gulf.
Permanent Resident Throughout Range.
For description, means of identification, food preferences, nest, habits, etc., etc., see page 133 of the Nature Library volume on BIRDS. For color markings and appearance in natural surroundings, see full-color illustration facing page 135.

Eagle, Bald

Parts of Country Where Found: United States; rare and local in California and in the arid interior.
Permanent Resident Throughout Range.
For description, means of identification, food preferences, nest, habits, etc., etc., see page 187 of the Nature Library volume on BIRDS.

Eagle, Golden

Parts of Country Where Found: Northern part of the Northern Hemisphere. Not found in Southern and Middle States; less common east of the Mississippi.
Permanent Resident Throughout Range.
For description, means of identification, food preferences, nest, habits, etc., etc., see page 187 of the Nature Library volume on BIRDS.

Grouse, Ruffed

Parts of Country Where Found: Eastern U. S. and southern Canada west to Minnesota, and south to Arkansas and northern Georgia.
Permanent but Roving Resident.
For description, means of identification, food preferences, nest, habits, etc., etc., see page 209 of the Nature Library volume on BIRDS. For color markings, and appearance in natural surroundings, see full-color illustration facing page 214.

Hawk, Sharp-shinned

Parts of Country Where Found: Breeds nearly throughout Canada and the U. S.; winters from British Columbia and Mass. to Panama. Same as Cooper's Hawk. Permanent resident except at northern limit of range.
For description, means of identification, food preferences, nest, habits, etc., etc., see page 193 of the Nature Library volume on BIRDS. For color markings and appearance in natural surroundings see full-color illustration facing page 194.

Hawk, Cooper's

Parts of Country Where Found: Breeds throughout temperate North America; winters in the U. S. and south to Costa Rica.
Permanent Resident, except at northern limits of range, where it is a summer or transient visitor.
For description, means of identification, food preferences, nest, habits, etc., etc., see page 193 of the Nature Library volume on BIRDS.

Hawk, Red-tailed

Parts of Country Where Found: Eastern North America, from southern Canada to eastern Texas and Florida.
Permanent Resident Throughout Range.
For description, means of identification, food preferences, nest, habits, etc., etc., see page 192 of the Nature Library volume on BIRDS.

Hawk, Red-shouldered

Parts of Country Where Found: Eastern North America from Manitoba and Nova Scotia to the Gulf States and Mexico, westward to Texas and the plains.
Permanent Resident Throughout Range.
For description, means of identification, food preferences, nest, habits, etc., etc., see page 190 of the Nature Library volume on BIRDS. For color, markings, and appearance in natural surroundings see full-color illustration facing page 175.

Jay, Blue

Parts of Country Where Found: North America east of the plains, from northern Canada to Florida and eastern Texas.
Permanent Resident. Although seen in flocks moving southward or northward, they are merely seeking happier hunting grounds, not migrating.
For description, means of identification, food preferences, nest, habits, etc., etc., see page 135 of the Nature Library volume on BIRDS. For color markings and appearance in natural surroundings see full-color illustration facing page 142.

Mocking-bird

Parts of Country Where Found: Southeastern U. S., north to eastern Nebraska, Ohio, and Maryland, and rarely to New York and Massachusetts.
No fixed migrations; *usually resident where seen*, except in the north.

FEBRUARY

For description, means of identification, food preferences, nest, habits, etc., etc., see page 52 of the Nature Library volume on BIRDS. For color, markings, and appearance in natural surroundings, see full-color illustration facing page 66.

Owl, Cat or Long-eared

Parts of Country Where Found: Breeds in southern Canada and northern U. S.; farther south in winter.
Usually a Permanent Resident.
For description, means of identification, food preferences, nest, habits, etc., etc., see page 179 of the Nature Library volume on BIRDS.

Owl, Screech

Parts of Country Where Found: Eastern North America.
Permanent Resident.
For description, means of identification, food preferences, nest, habits, etc., etc., see page 174 of the Nature Library volume on BIRDS. For color, markings, and appearance in natural surroundings, see full-color illustration facing page 166.

Owl, Barn

Pa ts of Country Where Found: U. S. rarely reaching Canada, south to Mexico. Nests from New York northward.
Permanent resident, except at northern limit of range.
For description, means of identification, food preferences, nest, habits, etc., etc., see page 180 of the Nature Library volume on BIRDS. For color, markings, and appearance in natural surroundings, see full-color illustration facing page 167.

Owl, Barred

Parts of Country Where Found: Eastern U. S. to Nova Scotia and Manitoba; west to Minnesota, Nebraska, Kansas, and Texas; nesting throughout range.
Permanent Resident.
For description, means of identification, food preferences, nest, habits, etc., etc., see page 176 of the Nature Library volume on BIRDS.

Sparrow, English

Parts of Country Where Found: Nearly the whole of Europe, and east to central Asia. Introduced and naturalized in America, New Zealand, Australia, etc.
Permanent Resident; does not migrate.

For description, means of identification, food preferences, nest, habits, etc., etc., see page 113 of the Nature Library volume on BIRDS. For color, markings, and appearance in natural surroundings, see full-color illustration facing page 114.

Titmouse, Tufted

Parts of Country Where Found: Nebraska and New Jersey to central Texas, the Gulf, and Florida. Casual farther north.
Permanent Resident in Its Range.
For description, means of identification, food preferences, nest, habits, etc., etc., see page 37 of the Nature Library volume on BIRDS. For color, markings, and appearance in natural surroundings, see full-color illustration facing page 39.

Woodcock

Parts of Country Where Found: Eastern North America, from British America to the Gulf, nesting nearly throughout its range; winters south of Virginia and southern Illinois.
Resident all but the coldest months; a few winter in north.
For description, means of identification, food preferences, nest, habits, etc., etc., see page 220 of the Nature Library volume on BIRDS.

Woodpecker, Red-headed

Parts of Country Where Found: U. S. east of the Rockies, except New England. North to Manitoba.
Migrations abundant but irregular.
For description, means of identification, food preferences, nest, habits, etc., etc., see page 160 of the Nature Library volume on BIRDS. For color, markings, and appearance in natural surroundings see full-color illustration facing page 151.

Woodpecker, Downy

Parts of Country Where Found: Eastern North America, from Labrador to Florida.
Resident all the year, throughout range.
For description, means of identification, food preferences, nest, habits, etc., etc., see page 164 of the Nature Library volume on BIRDS.

Woodpecker, Hairy

Parts of Country Where Found: Eastern North America from Canada to the Middle States.
Permanent Resident.

FEBRUARY

For description, means of identification, food preferences, nest, habits, etc., etc., see page 166 of the Nature Library volume on BIRDS.

Wren, Carolina

Parts of Country Where Found: Eastern U. S. Breeds from southeastern Nebraska and southern Pennsylvania to central Texas and northern Florida. Casual farther north.
Permanent Resident in Its Range.
For description, means of identification, food preferences, nest, habits, etc., etc., see page 47 of the Nature Library volume on BIRDS. For color, markings, and appearance in natural surroundings, see full-color illustration facing page 47.

GENERAL INDEX OF NAMES

GENERAL INDEX OF NAMES

Name	PAGE
Adder's tongue, Yellow	11
Alder, Seaside	143
Anemone, Star	57
Anemone, Wood	26
Arbutus, Trailing	11
Arethusa	47
Arrow-head, Broad-leaved	99
Ash, Eastern Mountain	63
Ash, Red	145
Ash, White	63
Aspen	14
Aster, Common blue, Branching, Wood, or Heart-leaved	134
Aster, Dense-flowered, White-wreathed or Starry	123
Aster, Golden	122
Aster, Large or Broad-leaved	123
Aster, Late Purple	123
Aster, Low, Showy, or Seaside Purple	123
Aster, New England	123
Aster, Red-stalked, Purple-stemmed or Early Purple	99
Aster, Smooth or Blue	134
Aster, White Heath	135
Aster, White Wood	124
Azalea, White or Clammy	81
Azalea, Wild	30
Azure, Spring	25
Badger, American	13
Baneberry, White	26
Barberry	47
Basswood	117
Bat, Little brown	137
Bear, Grizzly	118
Beard-tongue, Hairy	47
Beaver, Canadian	161
Bee balm	107
Beech, American	93
Beech-drops	124
Beech-drops, False	81
Beefsteak plant	27
Bellflower, Clasping	48
Bergamot, Wild	71
Betony, Wood	27
Bindweed, Blue	54
Bindweed, Hedge or Great	71
Bitterbloom	107
Bitter-buttons	110
Bittern	39
Bittersweet	54
Blackberry, High bush	48
Blackbird, Red-winged	8
Blackbird, Rusty	19
Black-bordered, Yellow	129
Black-eyed Susan	48
Bloodroot	26
Bluebird	8
Blue-eyed Grass, Pointed	48
Blue Flag, Larger, Fleur-de-lis	52
Blue, Scudders	86

Name	PAGE
Blue, Silvery	88
Blue, Tailed	89
Bluets	27
Blue-weed	72
Bobolink	39
Bob-white	168
Boneset	100
Bonnets	27
Bouncing Bet	71
Brooklime, American	27
Broom, Yellow or Indigo	76
Brown, Eyed	86
Buckeye	112
Bugloss, Vipers	72
Bunchberry	48
Bunting, Indigo	40
Burning Bush	144
Butter-and-eggs	124
Buttercup, Bulbous	49
Buttercup, Common meadow	49
Buttercup, Swamp or Marsh	27
Buttercup, Tufted	27
Butterfly-weed	72
Button-ball Shrub	72
Button-bush	72
Buzzard	168
Cabbage butterfly, White or Checkered	116
Cabbage butterfly, White or Imported	33
Calapogon	72
Camomile, Dogs or Fetid	100
Campion, Corn or Red	101
Campion, Starry	73
Canker-root	51
Cardinal	168
Cardinal Flower	105
Cardinal Flower, Blue	105
Caribou, Woodland	161
Carrion-flower	28
Carrot, Wild	73
Catbird	40
Catchfly	31
Celandine, Greater	28
Charlock	53
Chat, Yellow-breasted	40
Checker-berry	85
Checker-spot, Baltimore	87
Checker-spot, Harris'	87
Chickadee	40
Chickweed, Red	55
Chicory	100
Chipmunk	13
Cinquefoil, Common	29
Claytonia	12
Clapp	22
Clover, Common red	29
Clover, White Sweet	73
Clover, Yellow sweet	73
Clematis, Virginia	111
Clintonia, Yellow	49
Clover, White or Dutch	50

177

GENERAL INDEX OF NAMES

Name	PAGE
Cod-head	111
Cohosh	26
Cohosh, Black	74
Columbine, Wild	29
Comma, Gray	112
Comma	34
Comma, Green	59
Coot	41
Copper, American	89
Copper, Bronze	89
Corn cockle	101
Corn rose	101
Cornel, Silky	50
Cornel, Low or Dwarf	48
Corpse-plant	76
Cosmopolite	60
Cowbird	8
Cowslip, American	30, 32
Crane's bill	29
Cresent, Silver	86
Crow	169
Crowfoot, Tall	49
Cuckoos, Yellow- and Black-billed	19
Culver's-root	74
Daisy, Common, White, or Ox-eye	50
Daisy, Robert's Blue Spring	31
Daisy, Yellow or Ox-eye	48
Dandelion, Common	125
Dayflower, Virginia or Common	74
Deer, Virginia	14–66
Dodder, Gronovius' or Common	101
Dogbane, Spreading or Fly-trap	74
Dogs-head butterfly	89
Dogwood, Flowering	15, 28
Dogwood, Swamp	50
Dove, Mourning	9
Duck, Pintail	41
Duck, Shoveler	41
Dusky-wing, Persius's	34
Dusky-wing, Sleepy	112
Dutchman's Breeches	28
Eagle, Bald	169
Eagle, Golden	169
Eglantine	84
Elecampane	101
Elm, American	160
Elm, White	160
Emperor, Gray	86
Emperor, Goatweed	87
Emperor, Tawny	113
Everlasting, Pearly or Large-flowered	101
Field kale	53
Finch, Purple	9
Fire-weed, Great or Spiked	85
Five-finger	29
Fleabane, Daisy-leaved	31–50
Flicker	19
Flycatcher, Crested	41
Flycatcher, Least	42
Forget-me-not	51
Fox, Red	14
Foxglove, Downy false	102
Fringe Tree	64
Fritillary, Diana	129
Fritillary, Great Spangled	113
Fritillary, Gulf	90
Fritillary, Meadow	59
Fritillary, Mountain Silver-spot	87
Fritillary, Regal	113
Fritillary, Silver-bordered	60
Fritillary, Silver-spot	113
Fritillary, Variegated	89
Fritillary, White Mountain	89

Name	PAGE
Frost-flower	51
Frostweed, Hoary	75
Frost-weed, Long-branched	51
Frostwort	51
Garget	82
Gentian, Closed, Bottle, or Blind	125
Gentian, Fringed	135
Geranium, Wild or Spotted	29
Gerardia, Large Purple	125
Ghost-flower	76
Goldfinch	42
Gold-thread	51
Golden-rod, Blue-stemmed, Wreath or Woodland	125
Golden-rod, Canada	125
Golden-rod, Early, Plume, or Sharp-toothed	75
Golden-rod, Gray or Field	102
Golden-rod, Sweet	102
Golden-rod, White	103
Golden-rod, Wrinkle-leaved, or Tall or Hairy	103
Golden-rod, Zig-zag, or Broad-leaved	103
Goose, Canada	19
Grackles, Purple and Bronzed	9
Grass of Parnassus	107
Grass pink	72
Grosbeak, Rose-breasted	42
Ground-nut	103
Grouse, Ruffed	169
Gum, Sour, or Black	143
Gum, Sweet	143
Hairbell	75
Hair-streak, Acadian	114
Hair-streak, Banded	114
Hair-streak, Gray	114
Hair-streak, Great Purple	90
Hair-streak, Olive	60
Hair-streak, Striped	90
Hair-streak, White	90
Hardhack	103
Hare, Prairie	162
Harebell	75
Hawk, Cooper's	170
Hawk, Marsh	9
Hawk, Night	20
Hawk, Red-tailed	170
Hawk, Red-shouldered	170
Hawk, Sharp-shinned	169
Hawk, Sparrow	10
Hawkweed, Early or Vein-leaf	56
Hawkweed, Orange or Tawny	75
Hawthorn, Common	51
Heal-all	56
Hellebore, American White	52
Helmet-flower	109
Hemlock	64
Hepatica	12
Herb Robert	52
Heron, Great Blue	20
Heron, Little Green	20
Hog Apple	53
Honey-balls	72
Honeysuckle, Swamp	81
Honeysuckle, Wild, Pink, Purple	30
Hoodwort	109
Hop Merchant	34
Hornbeam, American	143
Horseheal	101
Horse-chestnut	64
Horse-weed	78
Hummingbird, Ruby-throated	42
Hyssop, Wild	84

GENERAL INDEX OF NAMES

Name	PAGE
Ice-plant	76
Indian paint	26
Indian paint-brush	55
Indian pipe	76
Indian poke	52
Indian root	109
Indigo, Wild	76
Ink-berry	82
Iris, Blue	52
Iron-weed	104
Jack-in-the-pulpit	30
Jamestown Weed	76
Jay, Blue	170
Jewel-weed	104
Jimson Weed	76
Jointweed	107
Joe-Pye-weed	126
Junco	154
Juvenal's, Dusky-wing	59
Kalmia, Broad-leaved	53
Killdeer	10
Kingbird	42
Kingfisher, Belted	10
Kinglet, Golden-crowned	21
Kinglet, Ruby-crowned	20
Knotweed, Pink	107
Lady's slipper, Large Yellow	52
Lady's slipper, Stemless	54
Ladies' tresses, Nodding	104
Laurell, Great	82–94
Laurel, Ground	11
Laurel, Mountain or American	53–94
Laurel, Narrow-leaved	77
Laurel, Sheep	77
Lettuce, Tall or Wild	78
Lily, Blackberry	77
Lily, Turk's cap	105
Lily, Red, Wood, or Flame	77
Lily, Sweet scented white pond	77
Lily, Water	77
Lily, Wild yellow, Meadow, Field or Canada	77
Linaria	57
Linden, American	117
Liver-leaf	12
Liverwort	12
Lobelia, Great	105
Lobelia, Red	105
Locust, Black	64
Locust, Honey	93
Loon	154
Loosestrife, Four-leaved or Whorled	78
Lousewort	27
Lynx, Canada	14
Magnolia, Starry	15
Mallow, Swamp Rose	126
Maple, Red	160
Maple, Sugar	144
Mandrake	53
Marigold, Marsh	30
Martin, Purple	21
Mayflower	11–51
May apple	53
Meadowlark	21
Meadow-rue, Early	30
Meadow-rue, Tall	106
Meadow-sweet	78
Melilot, White	73
Melilot, Yellow	73
Mesquite	64
Milfoil	85
Milkweed, Common	78
Milkweed, Orange	72

Name	PAGE
Milkwort, Common, Field, or Purple	79
Milkwort, Fringed	54
Moccasin flower, Pink, Venus'	54
Moccasin flower, Yellow	52
Mockernut,	65
Mocking-bird	170
Mole, Common	66
Monarch	88
Monkey-flower	79
Morning-glory, Wild	71
Mourning-cloak	13
Mother's heart	109
Motherwort	79
Mullein dock	79
Mullein, Great	79
Mullein, Moth	80
Muskrat	118
Mustard, Black	80
Mustard, Field or Corn	53
Mustard, Hedge	54
Nettle butterfly	61
New Jersey tea	54
Nightshade	54
Nuthatch, Red-breasted	155
Nuthatch, White-breasted	154
Oak, Post	161
Oak, Red	65
Oak, Scarlet	143
Oak, Shingle or Laurel	143
Oak, White	65
Orange-tip, Falcate	60
Orange-tip, Olympian	90
Orchis, Large, or Early, Purple-fringed	80
Orchis, Showy or Gay	30
Orchis, Yellow-fringed	106
Orchis, White-fringed	106
Oriole, Baltimore	43
Oriole, Orchard	43
Osprey	10
Oswego tea	107
Oven-bird	43
Owl, Barn	171
Owl, Barred	171
Owl, Cat or Long-eared	171
Owl, Screech	171
Owl, Short-eared	21
Painted Beauty	91
Painted Cup, Scarlet	55
Painted Lady	60
Palo Verde Acacia	35
Papilio, Short-tailed	91
Parnassian butterfly	129
Parsnip, Wild or Field	80
Partridge-berry	85
Partridge vine, Twin-berry	31
Peanut, Wild or Hog	127
Pearl crescent	112
Pearly eye	114
Pepperidge-bush	47
Persicaria, Common	107
Pewee, Wood	43
Phoebe	11
Physic	74
Pickerel-weed	81
Pigeon-berry	82
Pimpernel, Scarlet	55
Pine sap	81
Pine, White	65
Pink, Ground or Moss	31
Pink, Indian	47, 138
Pink, Rose	107
Pink, Sea or Marsh	108
Pink, Swamp	81

GENERAL INDEX OF NAMES

Name	PAGE
Pink, Wild	31
Pipsissewa	81
Pitcher Plant	55
Plant, Velvet or Flannel	79
Plantain, Robin's or Poor Robin's	31
Plover, Semipalmated or Ring-necked	43
Poke-weed	82
Polygala	54
Polygala, Purple	79
Pond lily, Large yellow	32
Poplar, Balsam	15
Primrose, Evening	82
Prince's pine	81
Prong-horn, American	94
Purple, Banded	114
Purple, Red-spotted	115
Quaker Ladies	27
Quail	168
Queen Anne's Lace	73
Rabbit, Snowshoe	162
Raccoon	66
Rail	22
Rail, Carolina or Sora	44
Raspberry, Purple-flowering or Virginia	82
Rattlesnake-weed	56
Red Admiral	61
Red Haw	51
Redbud	35
Redstart	44
Rhododendron, American or Great	82
Reindeer, American	161
Robin	11
Rockrose, Canadian	51
Rose Bay	94
Rose, Cherokee	127
Rose, Smoother, Early, or Meadow	83
Rose, Swamp	56
Sabbatia, Square-stemmed	107
Saint John's-wort, Common	83
Saint John's-wort, Great or Giant	108
Saint John's-wort, Shrubby	108
Sandpiper, Least	44
Sandpiper, Spotted	22
Sarsaparilla, Wild or False	56
Satyr, Arctic	91
Satyr, Little Wood	63
Saxifrage, Early	12
Scabious, Sweet	50
Scoke	82
Self-heal	56
Senna, Wild or American	109
Silver belltree	66
Silver-rod	103
Silkweed, Common	78
Sheepberry	35
Shepherd's purse	109
Shrike, Loggerhead	44
Shrike, Northern	155
Shooting star	32
Skipper, Least	91
Skipper, Long-tailed	91
Skipper, Roadside	61
Skipper, Silver-spotted	86
Skipper, Tawny-eyed	61
Skullcap, Larger or Hyssop	57
Skullcap, Mad-dog	109
Skunk	145
Skunk, or Swamp, Cabbage	12
Smartweed	107
Snake-head	111
Snakeroot, Black	74
Snap weed	104
Sneezeweed	128

Name	PAGE
Snowflake, or Snow Bunting	155
Soapwort	71
Solomon's Seal, False	57
Solomon's Seal, Hairy, or True	32
Sooty Wing	34
Sorrel Tree	117
Sparrow, Chipping	22
Sparrow, Field	155
Sparrow, English	171
Sparrow, Fox	156
Sparrow, Song	156
Sparrow, Swamp	156
Sparrow, Tree	156
Sparrow, Vesper	22
Sparrow, White-crowned	45
Speedwell, Common	56
Spignet	109
Spikenard	109
Spikenard, Wild	57
Spoonwood	56
Spring Beauty	12
Squirrel, Franklin Ground	94
Squirrel, Corn	83
Squirrel, Red	162
Star-flower	57
Star-grass, Yellow	57
Starwort, Yellow	101
Steeplebush	103
Succory	100
Sulphur, Brimstone or Cloudless	116
Sulphur, Cloud	116
Sulphur, Large Orange	91
Sulphur, Little	92
Sulphur, Orange	92
Sulphur, Pink-edged	92
Sumach, Dwarf	144
Sumach, Staghorn	144
Sundew, Round-leaved	110
Sunflower, Tall or Giant	128
Swallow, Bank	23
Swallow, Barn	22
Swallow, Tree	23
Swallowtail, Black	61
Swallowtail, Blue	116
Swallowtail, Giant	85
Swallowtail, Green-clouded	62
Swallowtail, Palamedes	62
Swallowtail, Tiger	62
Swallow-wort	28
Sunflower, Swamp	128
Sweetbrier	84
Swift, Chimney	23
Tanager, Scarlet	45
Tanager, Summer	23
Tansy	110
Tare	84
Thistle, Blue or Devil	72
Thistle butterfly	60
Thistle, Common, or Plumed, or Bull	110
Thistle, Pasture or Fragrant	110
Thorn apple	76
Thoroughwort	100
Thoroughwort, Purple	126
Thrasher, Brown	24
Titmouse, Tufted	172
Toadflax, Blue or Wild	57
Toadflax, Yellow	124
Tortoise-shell, American	92
Touch-me-not, Pale	111
Touch-me-not, Spotted	104
Towhee	24
Trillium, Painted	58
Trillium, Purple	32

GENERAL INDEX OF NAMES

Name	Page
Trout lily	11
Turtle-head	111
Veery	45
Venus' Looking-glass	48
Vervain, Blue	84
Vetch, Blue, Tufted or Cow	84
Vicereine	92
Viceroy	115
Violet, Birds-foot	58
"Violet," Dog-tooth	11
Violets, Downy and Smooth Yellow	33
Violets, White, Lance and Primrose-leaved and Sweet White	32
Violet-tip	62
Vireo, Red-eyed	24
Vireo, Warbling	45
Vireo, White-eyed	24
Virgin's bower	111
Vulture, Turkey	168
Wake-robin, Early or Dwarf	12
Wake-robin, Ill-scented	32
Wake-robin, Large-flowered	.58
Wake-robin, Nodding	58
Wake-robin, Painted	58
Wake-robin, Sessile-flowered	33
Walnut, Black	161
Walnut, Southwestern	145
Wanderer	92
Warbler, Black and White Creeping	25
Warbler, Blackburnian	.46
Warbler, Chestnut-sided	46
Warbler, Myrtle	24
Warbler, Yellow	46
Water lily	32
Waxwing, Cedar	157
Weatherglass or Clock, Poor Mans or Shepherd's	55
Whippoorwill	25
White, Great Southern	.93
White butterfly, Grey-veined	63
White Mountain butterfly	117
Willow-herb	85
Willow, Pussy	167
Willow, Weeping	15
Wind-flower	26
Wintergreen, Creeping	85
Witch-hazel	137, 144
Wood-nymph, The Common or Blue-eyed Grayling	117
Wood-nymph, The Southern	93
Woodcock	172
Woodchuck	167
Woodpecker, Downy	172
Woodpecker, Hairy	172
Woodpecker, Red-headed	172
Woodpecker, Yellow-bellied	25
Wood-sorrel, Violet	58
Wood-sorrel, White or True	59
Wren, Carolina	173
Wren, House	25
Wren, Marsh	46
Yarrow	85
Yellow-throat, Maryland	46
Zebra, butterfly	93
Zebra, swallowtail	34